AF696729

Computer Assisted Analytical Review System

Computer Assisted Analytical Review System

by
William R. Kinney, Jr.
(University of Michigan),
Gerald L. Salamon
(University of Iowa)
and
Wilfred C. Uecker
(Rice University)

American Accounting Association

Copyright, American Accounting Association, 1986. All rights reserved.
Library of Congress Catalog Card Number 85-073018
ISBN 0-86539-056-8
Printed in the United States of America

American Accounting Association
5717 Bessie Drive
Sarasota, FL 33583

CONTENTS

CONTENTS

List of Figures

Acknowledgments

This monograph was developed over a 2½-year period at the University of Iowa and the University of Michigan. It received financial support from The Touche Ross Foundation and technical support from Touche Ross & Co. partners and staff. We would like to thank Henry C. Korff and the Foundation as well as John Mullarkey, Kent Yarnall, and Ann Thornton of the Executive Office of Touche Ross and James Goodfellow of Touche Ross in Toronto.

We appreciate the programming assistance of Roger Jones and Kathy Lara of the University of Iowa, and especially Chris Westland of the University of Michigan.

We thank Don Madden of the University of Kentucky, Director of Education for the American Accounting Association, for his assistance. David Ricchiute of the University of Notre Dame, Larry Rittenburg of the University of Wisconsin, and Linda McDaniel of the University of Michigan provided many valuable comments and suggestions on the text and the diskette. Finally, we benefited greatly from the comments of our auditing students at the University of Iowa, the University of Michigan, and Rice University, who used early versions of the materials in class assignments.

Foreword

The Computer Assisted Analytical Review System (CAARS) is a set of programs and data designed to help you understand how to apply certain analytical review procedures used by practicing auditors. It should also help you understand some of the advantages and limitations of the procedures when applied many times under various conditions. A program called RATIO uses expected relationships among and between balance sheet and income statement components of monthly financial statements. A program called REGRN applies regression analysis to components of a single income statement account.

Chapter One of this booklet reviews the nature, timing, and extent of analytical review procedures as discussed in the authoritative auditing literature and introduces four approaches to analytical review—subjective, *ad hoc* rules, univariate statistical, and multivariate statistical. Error seeding and the CAARS approach are also discussed. Chapters Two and Three provide discussion of how the approaches have been operationalized by practicing auditors. Problem materials and computer instructions are provided for each approach. Chapter Two discusses approaches using financial statement ratio analysis and Chapter Three discusses approaches using regression analysis.

One

Analytical Review Procedures

Nature, Timing and Extent[1]

Nature of Analytical Review Procedures

According to *Statement on Auditing Standards* (SAS) *No. 23* (par. 2), analytical review procedures (ARPs) are "substantive tests of financial information made by a study and comparison of relationships among data." Thus, the procedures may result in professionally acceptable substantive evidence about a client's transactions and account balances. They are "reasonableness" tests of recorded amounts that may both increase the auditor's understanding of the client's business and provide audit evidence.

ARPs focus on summaries of transactions or subsidiary balances, in contrast to tests of details that focus on individual items. For example, an ARP might be applied to the year-end balances (i.e., at the annual financial statement level) by comparing the ratio of total recorded accounts receivable at year–end to recorded sales for the year with the ratio of audited values for the previous year. Also, even though the audit opinion relates to annual statement amounts, the auditor may find it useful to analyze changes in monthly financial statement ratios or monthly sales totals making up the sales balance for the year. On the other hand, tests of details of receivables and sales might include confirmation of individual balances with customers, or examination of particular sales documents or cash collections. Thus, while ARPs may provide evidence about the likelihood of monetary error in an account, tests of details are usually needed to confirm or deny that particular items are in error. ARPs provide less direct and less conclusive audit evidence about account validity.

Implicit in the auditor's analytical review procedures are his or her expectations of what the recorded amounts *should be* (that is, the

[1] This discussion draws heavily from Kinney and Felix [1980].

likely audited amount and the range of possible values that might reasonably be expected). For example, if gross profit has been about 60 percent of sales for the last several years and the auditor has no knowledge of changes in pricing policies, competitive conditions, or other economic factors, it would be reasonable to expect that the gross profit percentage for the current year would also be about 60 percent. The auditor probably would be unsatisfied if the gross profit based on current period book values was less than, say, 57 percent or more than, say, 64 percent, and would seek an explanation for such an unexpected change. Similarly, a time-series regression analysis of monthly sales regressed against a measure of monthly sales for the client's industry may reveal months in which book values are far from the expected audited amounts given the industry sales for the months.

The auditor faces four possible outcomes depending on his or her investigation decision and the true state of an account balance. The auditor who decides not to investigate an account may have 1) correctly decided not to investigate an account that is correct within acceptable limits, or 2) made a type II error (i.e., not investigated an account that is not within acceptable limits). The auditor who decides to investigate may have 1) correctly decided to investigate an account that is not within acceptable limits, or 2) made a type I error (i.e., investigated an account that is within acceptable limits). Figure 1 shows the cross-classification of outcomes. As shown in Figure 1, the auditor is subject to only one error for each possible state of the balance.

The cost to the auditor of a type I error is the needless search for error and the possible loss of client goodwill due to the unnecessary

FIGURE 1

POSSIBLE INVESTIGATION DECISION AND ERROR CONDITION OUTCOMES

	Error Condition	
Investigation Decision	Accounting Error is Within Acceptable Limits	Accounting Error is not Within Acceptable Limits
Do Not Investigate:	Correct Decision	Type II Error
Investigate:	Type I Error	Correct Decision

increase in the cost of the audit. For analytical review, the cost to the auditor of a type II error is related to the increase in the risk of failing to detect material error and incorrectly reporting upon financial statements that are materially in error. These costs include out-of-pocket costs for legal defense, actual damage settlements, and increases in liability insurance premiums. Of more importance is the cost of a damaged professional reputation for the audit firm.

Two uses of analytical review procedures are described in *SAS No. 23* (par. 3). The analytical review "may indicate the need for additional procedures or may indicate that the extent of other auditing procedures may be reduced." The first use might be called "attention directing." It focuses on the identification of unusual or unexpected recorded amounts or relationships among such amounts. Unusual recorded amounts might be caused by factors such as the following:

a. the presence of accounting errors;
b. the presence of accounting irregularities;
c. a change in the accounting principles used;
d. changes in business conditions;
e. the occurrence of unusual events during the period.

Each of these causes may have audit significance and early identification may be valuable to the auditor.

According to *SAS No. 23* (par. 8-10), the auditor should investigate unusual fluctuations identified by ARPs. In conducting such "analytical" investigations, the auditor ordinarily begins with an inquiry of management. In considering management's explanations the auditor should "evaluate the reasonableness of replies to his inquiries by reference to his knowledge of the business and other information. . . ." The auditor must guard against "truncating" the analytical investigation by accepting a seemingly plausible explanation that may conflict with his or her other knowledge. We consider the analytical investigation truncation problem in Chapter Two.

Once the cause of an unusual amount has been identified (or, indeed, if no such cause can be determined), the auditor may decide that a particular transaction cycle or balance needs more audit attention than was originally planned. This increased audit attention could take the form of increased tests of details or additional analytical review procedures later in the audit, and might eventually lead to an audit adjustment, additional disclosures, or a qualified opinion.

If the auditor plans to use ARPs to relax other planned tests of details, the second use of the procedures—the "tests-of-details substitute"—is applicable. Substituting evidence from ARPs for tests of details is inherently more risky than employing such evidence to identify areas requiring special or more than normal auditing. Therefore, the auditor should carefully consider whether to restrict planned audit tests on the basis of the reasonableness of recorded amounts. When ARPs are used as a test-of-details substitute, it may be necessary to conduct the error search to find "intolerable" error (the amount of error just in excess of "tolerable" error for the account as defined in *SAS No. 39* (par. 18)). ARP conclusions then can be more easily incorporated into a substantive audit sampling plan that is designed to detect intolerable error if it exists.

While the *lack* of expected relationships should cause the auditor to extend planned tests, whether the converse is true may be the subject of considerable debate. For example, internal accounting controls may not be adequate to detect irregularities and may allow amounts to be intentionally manipulated to yield the expected results. Similarly, the inability to independently corroborate management's explanation of relationships will affect the reliance that is justified. When used with care, however, ARPs can provide valuable substantive audit evidence.

In concept, analytical review procedures can be applied simultaneously to identify fluctuations in either an upward or downward direction. In practice, however, ARPs are usually applied to one direction at a time. This is because most follow-up procedures depend upon the direction of an identified change. An unusual increase in sales, for example, may cause the auditor to consider the possibility that some recorded sales are fictitious while such an explanation would not be considered if recorded sales is unexpectedly small. This consideration of specific types of possible errors is consistent with the auditor's consideration of particular errors or irregularities that might occur when studying and evaluating the client's system of internal accounting control (*SAS No. 1,* section 320, par. 69). For these reasons, in the problems of Chapters Two and Three, we shall consider only fluctuations that are consistent with the *overstatement of the earnings* of the client firm.

Timing of Analytical Review Procedures

In considering the varying objectives that are appropriate for analytical review procedures, *SAS No. 23* lists the following combinations of timing and objectives:

a. In the initial planning stages to assist in determining the nature, extent, and timing of other auditing procedures by identifying, among other things, significant matters that require consideration during the examination.
b. During the conduct of the examination in conjunction with other procedures applied by the auditor to individual elements of financial information.
c. At or near the conclusion of the examination as an overall review of the financial information.

These time frames will determine, in large part, how the auditor will use ARPs and the type of procedure that is best suited to the purpose. For example, in the planning stages, the auditor will be planning tests of details as well as other ARPs for the remainder of the audit. ARPs at the planning stage will more likely be attention-directing and may be rather imprecise in signalling error. Similarly, at the end of the audit, the auditor uses ARPs to direct attention to any remaining unusual relationships. During the examination the auditor may find more precise ARPs, such as regression analysis, useful as a test of details substitute.

Extent of Analytical Review Procedures

It may be relatively difficult to vary the extent to which a particular ARP is employed. Since these procedures consider overall relationships in assessing the reasonableness of a recorded amount, the auditor cannot determine overall reasonableness by examining a small part of the relationships. Conversely, when an overall evaluation has been made, it may be difficult to extend the test. For example, one may not be able to get a "larger sample" by dividing the data into smaller slices using monthly or weekly data because the relative magnitude of accounting "cutoff" errors is likely to be quite large and may mislead the auditor.

Another constraint on the extent of the procedures is that it may not be possible to improve the precision or "closeness" of predictions because the relationships change over time. Relationships that existed in 1979 may be of little value in assessing the reasonableness of recorded amounts in the latter 1980s.

Thus, the extent of a particular ARP tends to be relatively fixed. The auditor must do enough work to assess the overall reasonableness of recorded amounts. If the resulting evaluation is that more evidence is needed, the auditor often will have to turn to other auditing procedures.

To sum up, there are two uses for ARPs, and as many as three times at which they might be applied. The *attention-directing* use causes little controversy as an audit procedure. Any procedure that might direct attention to areas of likely error is potentially valuable. For attention directing, the type I error risk (the risk of incorrectly rejecting a materially correct balance) is increased and the type II error risk (the risk of incorrectly accepting a materially in-error balance) is decreased. However, the *tests-of-details-substitute* use presents some practical as well as conceptual difficulties because the type I error risk may be decreased and the type II error risk may be increased. In audit sampling, the auditor can control both type I and type II error risks by varying the sample size. Since the auditor may not be able to vary the "sample size" for ARPs, only one of these risks can be controlled and the other risk left to vary.

Even if the auditor feels confident about the reliability of a procedure, how can such feelings be converted into a revision of planned tests of details and other auditing procedures? Although ARPs draw on the auditor's business expertise and knowledge of client activities, how does the auditor determine when such information is useful? How can the auditor best use such information and his or her analytical skills in forming expectations as to likely audited values? We consider these questions in the discussion to follow.

Approaches to Analytical Review

There are several approaches to analytical review. They differ as to *inputs* (the data required and the way that the data are transformed into an expected audited value), and *outputs* (the assessed reliance to be placed on ARP results and the degree to which the results can be verified objectively by others).

The ideal approach would require little information, involve simple transformation methods, and yield precise, reliable expectations of audited values that can be verified objectively by others. Unfortunately, precise, reliable answers usually require a great variety of timely, detailed, and often expensive data. Also, precise, objectively verifiable results usually require relatively complex processing methods. The best choice in a particular audit application usually involves a trade-off between what might loosely be called the "precision" of expectations that are developed and the cost of obtaining the precision.

Present knowledge of the performance of different methods of analytical review under various circumstances is quite limited. There are, however, several characteristics of different analytical review methods which can serve as a guide to the auditor. By considering the different data and transformation methods required, we can see some of the risks as well as advantages of the use of alternative methods of analytical review. Below we describe four approaches to analytical review commonly employed by auditors and discuss the relative advantages of each. These approaches are: subjective evaluation, *ad hoc* rules, univariate statistical, and multivariate statistical.

Subjective Evaluation

The original analytical review approach, and probably the most widely used today, is simply a subjective evaluation of an account balance or ratio of account balances by an expert auditor. Applying professional judgment and drawing on knowledge of the client's specific environmental data, the auditor may determine a reasonable range of values for the audited balance. Since all the auditor's knowledge of the client can be incorporated in this judgment, the auditor may be very confident about the assessed range for the audited balance. The auditor may consider data that are external to the company, such as local bank deposits, gross national product measures, and employment rates, and internal data, such as production records, related account balances, and budgeted amounts (reflecting management's expectations). Also, knowledge of past audits may indicate which balances are most likely to contain errors. For example, with his or her knowledge of local wage and unemployment rates, the auditor of a retail store might consider the joint reasonableness of recorded accounts receivable with the related sales, cash collections, and inventory levels. Thus, the auditor's subjective approach can, in effect, be "multivariate" in nature. Specific events, such as wildcat strikes, adverse weather conditions, construction problems, or installation of new equipment, can be conveniently considered. The primary advantage of the subjective method is the ability to use any data available.

In the context of financial ratio analysis, the auditor may assess the reasonableness of each ratio. Also, the auditor may search for patterns in the financial ratios. For example, an omitted purchase of materials on account (the client fails to record a purchase and the related liability) decreases the inventory turnover ratio and the ratio of cost of sales to sales, but increases the raw materials to accounts payable ratio. The auditor may simultaneously evaluate more than one account or ratio; thus, when employed by an experienced auditor, the subjective approach can be very effective.

The major problem with the subjective method is its subjective nature—other persons, perhaps with different perspectives or at a different time, may see the same "facts" as implying a different conclusion. The other persons may be fellow auditors, an investor who has lost money, or witnesses for the plaintiff in court. Different "experts" may see the same conditions as yielding far different reasonable values, and thus make different subjective assessments of the reliance to be placed on analytical review results. Similarly, knowing that a firm has failed may change even the same person's assessment of the implications of ARP results. Furthermore, even though senior auditors may be able to form consistent and reliable expectations, juniors may not be able to do so. Thus, while part of a senior's skill may, of course, be subject to routinization analogous to data editing programs scanning and editing an EDP file for quantitatively "unusual" transactions or balances, many difficulties remain in effective training for the subjective approach to analytical review.

Ad hoc Rules

A second approach to analytical review consists of what might be called "rules of thumb." Rules are specified which use relatively simple quantitative relationships such as comparing ratios of prior years' audited values with the current audit year's recorded amounts. Rather than making a formal prediction of audited value, the auditor merely decides to investigate if the difference between years exceeds some preset "critical value." An example is the investigation rule: "Investigate if the current year's ratio based on book values differs from last year's audited ratio by more than ten percent."

The use of this method has support in the professional standards literature including *SAS No. 21, SAS No. 22, SAS No. 23,* and *SAS No. 36* as well as in practice-oriented materials (e.g., Smith [1983]). Furthermore, recent empirical research studies suggest that this method may be fairly effective in predicting adjustments (e.g., Kinney [1979] and Hylas and Ashton [1982]).

Ad hoc rules also have the advantage of being objective in the sense that their results can be reproduced by others and, like the subjective method, they are easy to apply. Unlike the subjective method, however, they focus on a single account or ratio. Furthermore, the specification of the best "critical value" is highly subjective. Finally, neither the subjective method nor the *ad hoc* rule permit an objective statistical calculation of both predictions and ranges of reasonable values. Therefore, neither affords an objective, verifiable measure of the reliability of the analytical review results and may reduce their usefulness as a test of details substitute.

Univariate Statistical Models

This approach uses past audited values of a single account or ratio (or values from other firms) to assess the probability distribution of possible audited values for the audit period. With the distribution of expected audited values or the distribution of changes in expected audited values, an objective statistical confidence interval can be constructed. Knowledge of the industry distribution will usually allow much more precise assessments. Suppose, for example, that changes in the audited Accounts Receivable Turnover ratio follow a normal distribution. Other things equal, the probability that the absolute change in a particular firm's ratio will be greater than 2.0 standard deviations is less than .05. Such a large change probably should be investigated to rule out accounting error as the cause.

Univariate statistical methods allow objective calculation of both the predicted value of a ratio of audited account balances and a range of reasonable values. If the ratio or changes in the ratio follow an identifiable probability distribution, reliable probability statements may be possible. A disadvantage of the method is that too much attention may be paid to single ratios and too little attention to broader patterns or the "overall picture" of the client firm. Also, because conditions change over time, a time-series confidence interval using only the client firm's past audited values may not be satisfactory. Consequently, it will usually be desirable for the auditor to obtain additional information, such as industry data, that will permit assessment of the cross-sectional distribution of audited values or changes in audited values.

Multivariate Statistical Models

A fourth approach uses statistical regression models to relate the account balance to environmental variables that are theoretically related to the account balance or cause the account balance to vary.

For example, cost of sales may be related to the number of units sold for the period, to a price index based on prices paid for major materials components of the product, and to current-period wage rates. The auditor can gather data on *past* costs of sales, units sold, price indexes, and wage rates and determine the usual relationship between cost of sales and the "causal" or "independent" variables. Then, by inserting audit year values of the independent variables, the auditor can use the past relationship to determine estimates of the audited cost of sales for the audit period. This is quite different from a simple time-trend extrapolation because it allows objective consideration of current audit year values of the quantity, price, and wage factors.

Regression analysis has been used as an ARP by several audit firms. The explanatory power of regression-based structural models in auditing can be quite high. Correlations of .90 or above are relatively common. This implies that about 81 percent of the variation in an account balance can often be explained by environmental information. More important, the "standard errors" of the estimates (which are measured in dollars) are often sufficiently small relative to tolerable or material error that the regression results may allow a substantial reduction in planned substantive tests of details.

As with univariate statistical models, multivariate statistical models allow objective calculation of both predictions and ranges of reasonable values. Hence, both have the advantage of an objective, verifiable measure of the reliability of the analytical review results. The multivariate regression method typically gives more precise estimates of audited values than do univariate methods. This property means accounting errors are easier to see and that multivariate methods are more likely to be useful as a test-of-details substitute. However, the multivariate method may involve considerable costs in developing accurate data for use in the regression model, and ordinarily requires the use of a computer program to make the regression estimates and calculations of the investigation decision rule. The availability of inexpensive time-shared computer programs as well as microcomputers has greatly reduced the latter problem.

Another advantage of regression analysis of an account balance is that the auditor can compare the amount of unexpected fluctuation with a measure of materiality. This was not possible in ratio analysis for two reasons. First, in the analysis of a ratio of two numbers, a "reasonable" change in the numerator (denominator) depends on the value of the denominator (numerator), and either of the numbers may be in error. The two possibilities for error, and the variation due to their division, make comparisons with a single materiality number difficult. Second, the standard error of prediction using only past changes in a ratio is usually too high for audit reliance. In regression analysis of a single account, however, the first problem does not apply and the standard error of prediction using regression is often small enough for audit reliance. Thus, regression analysis allows the auditor to specify materiality and the type II error risk and to measure the type I error risk. Regression analysis still doesn't allow the auditor to vary the "amount" of evidence or the regression "sample size," of course. The latter capability allows the auditor applying audit sampling to set the type I and type II error risks as well as materiality and vary the sample size to control all three.

Figure 2 summarizes the prediction and reliability characteristics of the four approaches discussed above. In Chapter Two we illustrate the first three methods in the context of financial ratio analysis. In Chapter Three we illustrate the regression approach.

FIGURE 2

SUMMARY CHARACTERISTICS OF ANALYTICAL REVIEW METHODS

Method	Information Used	Predictions Determined	Reliability of Predictions Determined
Subjective	Any available information	Subjectively	Subjectively
Ad hoc rules	Past audited values	Objectively	Subjectively
Univariate statistical	Past audited values	Objectively	Objectively
Multivariate statistical (regression)	Past audited values and quantifiable environmental information	Objectively	Objectively

Computer Assisted Analytical Review System (CAARS)

The Computer Assisted Analytical Review System (CAARS) is a set of programs and data designed to help you understand the application, advantages, and limitations of certain analytical review procedures used by practicing auditors. A program called RATIO uses balance sheet and income statement data from an actual company to conduct financial ratio analysis as an attention director. A program called REGRN uses simulated income statement account data based on real-world parameters to conduct regression analysis as a test-of-details substitute. The programs and data sets are contained on a single diskette and run on IBM PC and compatible microcomputers with 256K memory.

Both RATIO and REGRN are composed of four types of data and four subprograms to combine and process the data. Both require you to enter critical values to guide the program in selecting balances to be analytically investigated and both allow you to make modifications to the data. Figure 3 is a diagram of the components of CAARS and how they are interrelated.

As shown in Figure 3, the Prediction Model Program takes audited values from the base period (prior audit years) and industry data from prior years as well as the current audit year to "predict" the current audit year's audited values. Book values are *created* by the Error Seeding Program. That is, audited values (or values that are assumed to be error-free) for the current audit year are seeded with accounting errors specified by the program (or by you). By creating book values with known "accounting errors," you can see the ability of the analytical review procedures to detect errors.

The Error Identification Program computes the difference between the book values and the predicted audited values. The difference is compared with the critical value specified by you (the auditor). Balances that are identified as excessive or unusual are written out for analytical investigation. Finally, the Error Analysis Program compares the balances to be investigated with the actual errors seeded. While a practicing auditor will ordinarily not know whether all material accounting error has been detected, you will know the amount and location of errors that have been seeded. Therefore, you can assess the ability of an analytical review procedure to correctly identify the seeded accounting errors as well as the frequency of type I and type II errors.

To run CAARS, insert the Disk Operation System (DOS) diskette for your microcomputer into the disk drive. When the DOS has been loaded, remove the diskette and insert the CAARS diskette. (If you have two disk drives, insert the CAARS diskette into drive A.) Enter the letters 'CAARS' and press the return key. This will bring up the CAARS program and it will ask you for the input necessary to run all parts of the program. For example, the first question asked is which program you wish to run. You should enter RATIO if you want to use the Financial Ratio Analysis Module and you should enter REGRN if you want to use the Regression Analysis Module.

Good Luck!

FIGURE 3

DIAGRAM OF *CAARS*

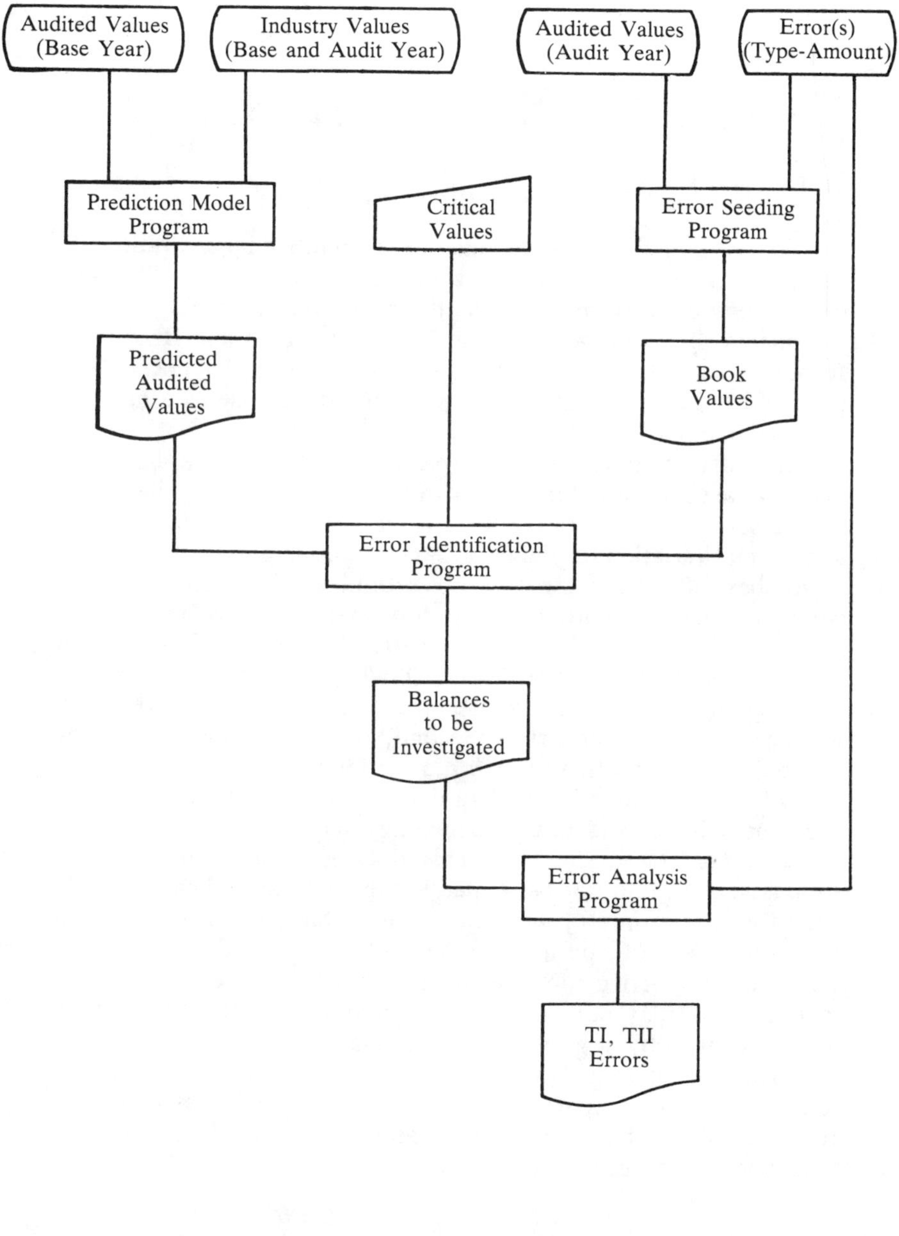

Two

Financial Ratio Analysis Module

Introduction

In assessing the reasonableness of a client's financial ratios, the auditor may make comparisons with industry ratios as well as with ratios computed from the client's prior year audited financial statements. Industry ratios are available from Dun and Bradstreet, Robert Morris Associates, and other publishers of financial data. Many CPA firms purchase these publications for use as a basis for industry comparisons in their audits.

Industry comparisons may be particularly beneficial as indicators of potential business failure and as an aid to understanding the client's business. Industry statistics provide a measure of average performance and normal variation for the period. For auditing purposes, however, a number of factors limit their usefulness. First, since no two companies are the same, the comparisons are not always meaningful. For example, if your client is a consistently "high performer" or a consistently "low performer," your client's financial ratios may always differ significantly from the industry mean. This will be true even in the absence of accounting error. Second, different companies follow different accounting methods. If most companies in the industry use FIFO inventory valuation and straight-line depreciation, while your client uses LIFO and double-declining-balance depreciation, comparisons may be misleading. This does not mean that industry comparisons should not be made. Rather, it is an indication of the need for care in interpreting the results. Third, there is a time lag between the end of a period and the publication of industry statistics. The data may arrive too late to be useful to the auditor. Finally, industry data may not be measured in sufficient detail as to time period, geographic region, or account classification.

An alternative to the use of industry ratios as a basis for comparison is to compare the audit period ratios with those of prior audit years for the client. Arens and Loebbecke [1980] list the following advantages for this approach.

1. There are no restrictions on the number and type of calculations to make. For most comparisons to industry sources there are a limited number of ratios published.
2. The ratios can be much more specific and directly related to the auditor's areas of interest. For example, when the auditor wants to calculate sales returns and allowances on a monthly basis, it is possible to do so if the data are available in the records.
3. The comparisons are made only within the firm; therefore, there is no problem of determining the client's industry.
4. There is little difficulty encountered in comparing data based upon different methods of accounting. In fact, one of the uses of analytical testing is discovering instances where the client has changed accounting methods without disclosing this fact in the financial statements.

In the Financial Ratio Analysis Module, we follow a composite approach. That is, you will compare monthly ratios for a sample firm with data from its own past, adjusted for the median change for the firm's industry. As will be discussed below, monthly statements are analyzed because of the difficulty in detecting material errors in the more highly aggregated annual financial statements. Actual month-end balances have been obtained for five recent calendar (audit) years. The sample firm is a wholesale distributor. It has relatively good internal accounting controls and uses the first-in, first-out method and a periodic count system for inventory and cost of sales. Independent personnel make test counts of about one-12th of the inventory each month to estimate the total ending inventory. There have been no changes of accounting methods over the five-year period.

To simulate current year *unaudited* values, the account balances of your test month may have been "seeded" with one of two types of accounting error described below. The amount of the error, if any, will be the amount designated as "material" for the client (see *SAS No. 47*, paragraph .04).

A recent AICPA study of practicing auditors' judgments about materiality showed that the revenues of a firm are highly correlated with their auditor's judgments about materiality [Warren, 1983]. For relatively small firms, one-half of one percent of sales was a good approximation to auditors' assessments of materiality. For this module, we define a material amount as .005 × sales of the previous audit year adjusted by the approximate expected growth rate for sales for the client's industry—about eight percent. That is, materiality = .005 × last year's (audited) sales × 1.08. Any error in the income statement accounts will be closed to retained earnings each month, but the balance sheet accounts will continue to reflect the error throughout the rest of the audit year since we are assuming that the error has not yet been discovered.

The assumption of an error of a material amount in a single month is somewhat unrealistic, of course. Single errors of such a large amount are rare for firms with good internal accounting controls. A more likely condition for materially-in-error financial statements would be multiple errors, spread over several months. Such dispersed errors and strategies for detecting them will be considered in the Regression Analysis Module to follow.

In the present module, your task is to assess the reasonableness of selected ratios of the sample firm. The type of concentrated error, if any, that has been seeded is unknown to you. To minimize the data-gathering and computation effort involved, the selection of the audit month, specification of the audit year, and values of selected account balances and ratios will be provided to you by the computer when you run the program. Specific ratios employed are described below.

Financial Ratios Used

Selected account balances related to the basic purchasing and sales cycle of the wholesaling firm are used. The selection criterion is the ability of a ratio to reflect changes that could be attributed to accounting error overstating earnings. Typical ratios used for financial analysis are not always useful for this purpose. Consequently, some of the ratios employed here may be unfamiliar to you. The ratios are:

1) Accounts Receivable Turnover = $$\frac{\text{SALES}}{\text{ACCOUNTS RECEIVABLE}}$$

2) Inventory Turnover = $$\frac{\text{COST OF SALES}}{\text{INVENTORY}}$$

3) Cost of Sales Ratio = $$\frac{\text{COST OF SALES}}{\text{SALES}}$$

4) Accruals Ratio = $$\frac{\text{ACCOUNTS RECEIVABLE}}{\text{ACCOUNTS PAYABLE}}$$

The first two ratios relate an income statement or "flow" account to a balance sheet or "stock" account. The third ratio relates two income statement accounts. *A priori,* the third ratio is likely to be a ratio with high diagnosticity (i.e., able to facilitate correct "diagnosis" of a problem) since management often plans and operates a business with an equilibrium or a target Cost of Sales Ratio in mind. Furthermore, if sales are low relative to expectations, then the related cost of sales is frequently down by a similar proportion. The last ratio relates one balance sheet account to another. It measures the amounts owed to the firm in relation to the amount the firm owes. Thus it measures an aspect of liquidity and is, of course, a component of the traditional working capital or "current" ratio. We have separated it for purposes of analysis since combining receivables with other current assets would lower the ability to detect some types of errors. For example, an error that overstates receivables would have the same effect on the current ratio as would an error overstating inventory.

The ratios will be computed for your client's book values for all 12 months of the audit year as well as for the audited values of each month of the prior year (the base period). In contrast to the calculation you may have used in finance classes, *ending* balances rather than average balances are used in computing all ratios. The use of ending balances is desirable from an audit perspective because it isolates potential errors in the current period book amounts from the prior period amounts. For example, if ending inventory this month is materially overstated, averaging the beginning inventory balance (which is correct) with the ending inventory balance in computing the inventory turnover ratio would about halve the overstatement, thus making the ending inventory error harder to detect.

The Investigation Decision

In the financial ratio analysis module, you will use analytical review as an "attention director" (see *SAS No. 23,* par. .05 and .09). After studying your client's ratios, making relevant comparisons, and following up exceptions with an "analytical" investigation or inquiry, you must decide whether the client's recorded (book) values may be materially in error and thus warrant exceptional audit attention in subsequent internal control study and evaluation or substantive tests.

The problem of identifying particular account balances that are in error is complex. Each ratio involves two accounts; consequently, if the ratio seems unreasonable, you must investigate at least one of the two component account balances. Since an error may affect more than one ratio, the number of accounts to be investigated can be large. Thus the likelihood of making at least some type I or type II errors can also be large. However, the cost of obtaining a satisfactory explanation in an "analytical investigation" of an account that is, in fact, error-free may be small. Therefore, a fairly high rate of type I errors may be tolerated.

Error Conditions

If an error is seeded, it will be one of the following types.

A. Omitted Purchases on Account—Material purchases for resale and the corresponding accounts payable have not been recorded. (Assume that the goods have been sold during the test month.)

B. Fictitious Charge Sales—Material credit sales and the corresponding accounts receivable have been fraudulently recorded for nonexistent credit sales transactions.

Each of these error conditions materially affects book values of accounts that typically require adjustment during the course of an audit [Kinney, 1979 and Hylas and Ashton, 1982]. The effects on the accounts and related financial ratios are described below.

Omitted Purchases on Account: Both purchases and accounts payable will be understated by the amount of the unrecorded purchase. As a result, cost of sales will be understated and net income before taxes (NIBT) will be overstated. Three of the four ratios will be affected by this error. The direction of the effect is indicated in the middle column of Figure 4. You should verify that the direction analysis is correct and be able to explain your reasoning. Figure 5 extends the analysis by plotting the effect of a material error on the expected values of the ratios based on relative magnitudes of actual data for the test firm. Figure 5 assumes that there are no "random" or non-accounting error fluctuations. The ratio values are measured in standardized (i.e., standard deviation) units.

If accounting error is large enough relative to the balances and normal variation (i.e., a high ratio of the accounting error "signal" to the random variation "noise"), then all three ratios should move in the predicted direction. As shown in Figure 5, panel a, however, two of the three ratios (ratios 2 and 4) are not much affected by material omitted purchases. Thus, the ease with which a "material" error can be detected by looking for fluctuations in ratios depends, in part, on

FIGURE 4

LIKELY DIRECTION OF CHANGE IN MONTH OF ERROR FOR SELECTED ERRORS

	Error	
Ratio	Omitted Credit Purchase	Fictitious Credit Sale Entered
1. Accounts Receivable Turnover: (Sales/Accts. Rec.)	—	Up*
2. Inventory Turnover: (Cost of Sales/Inv.)	Down	—
3. Cost of Sales Ratio: (Cost of Sales/Sales)	Down	Down
4. Accruals Ratio: (Accts. Rec./Accts. Pay.)	Up	Up

*Up since, for the test company, this ratio is always less than 1.

error size in relation to the sizes and normal variation of the component account balances comprising the ratio.

Fictitious Credit Sales Recorded: Both sales and accounts receivable will be overstated by the amount of fictitious sales recorded. As a result, NIBT and total assets will also be overstated. Three of the four ratios are affected by this error. The direction of the effect for the month of entry is indicated in the right-most column of Figure 4.

Figure 5, panel b, shows that the cost of sales ratio "spike" for the error month is smaller for fictitious sales than it is for omitted purchases. This is because sales is larger than cost of sales and the effect of subtraction (addition) of a *given* amount from (to) the numerator (denominator) depends on the base amount to which it is subtracted (added).

One could extend the analysis of Figure 5 to months after the error and look for patterns based on the accounts with errors that carry forward. For example, while a fictitious sale will be closed to income each month, ratios involving receivables will remain misstated as long as receivables are overstated. While such an analysis is possible, it is not likely to be fruitful since the magnitudes of the difference in ratios for months subsequent to the error are quite small and the effect is difficult to see.

FIGURE 5

STANDARDIZED ERROR PATTERN
$((r_t - \hat{r}_t)/s_r)$
WITH ERROR BEGINNING AT MONTH 4

Panel a.

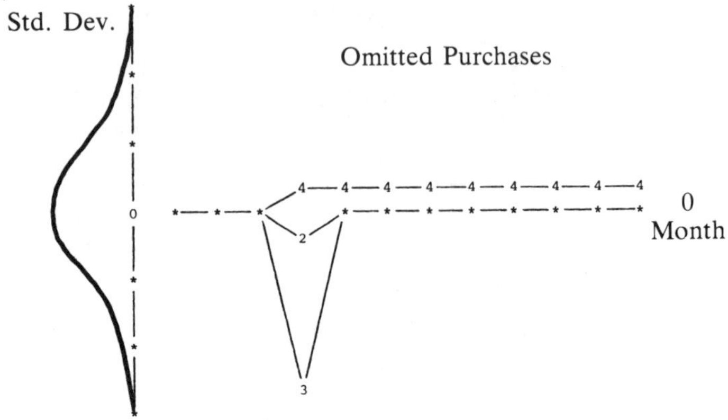

Ratios: 1 = Accounts Receivable Turnover
2 = Inventory Turnover
3 = Cost of Sales Ratio
4 = Accruals Ratio

Panel b.

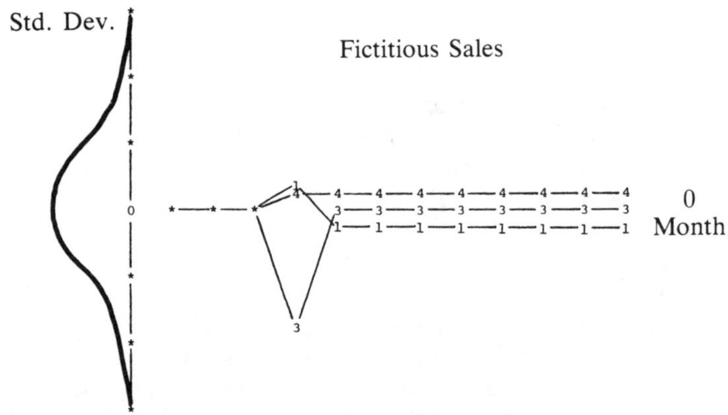

Panel c.

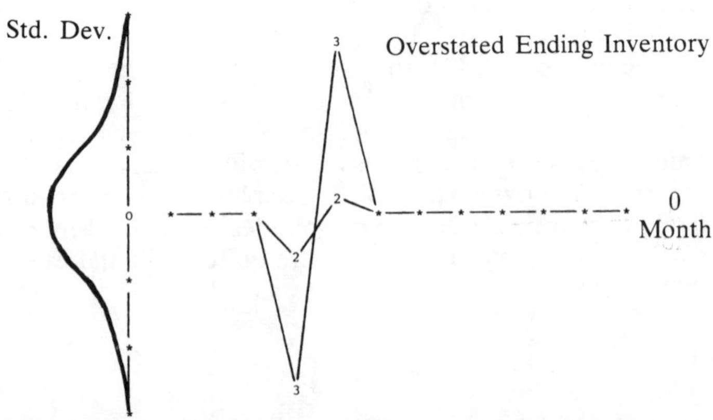

In contrast to the two types of errors studied, an ending inventory counting or pricing error affects income for the month subsequent to the error. For example, if the month-end inventory is overstated due to overcounting the ending stock, the error month's cost of sales will be understated and both NIBT and total assets will be overstated (see Figure 5, panel c). If the subsequent inventory is counted correctly, then the cost of sales for the subsequent month will be *overstated* by the same amount of the understatement during the month of the miscount. This will show up as a large negative spike in the Cost of Sales ratio in the error month followed by a large positive spike the next month. An undercount has the opposite pattern. For some months the client's ratios based on audited values exhibit such patterns. This implies that even though the data have been audited each year (and the annual balances probably are not materially misstated), there may still be some rather large counting errors in the monthly balances. If the year-end inventory is correct, however, the cost of sales for the *year* will be correct.

Financial Ratio Problems

Phase I—Analysis of a Single Fiscal Month

Phase I consists of two problems that test your ability to conduct an analytical review of account balances as of the end of a particular fiscal month. Each of you will probably receive a different audit month and/or year when you run CAARS. Furthermore, you may not all receive the same error condition. Consequently, you will have to work independently on this assignment.

The computer will provide the following information about your client. (Examples of items 1-4 are shown in Figure 6 and an example of item 5 is shown in Figure 7.)

1. The four ratios and related account balances for the test month of the year under audit. These amounts are unaudited.
2. The four ratios and related account balances for the client for the month prior to the test month, the test month of the prior year, and the average and standard deviation for the 12 months of the prior year. The prior year amounts are audited and the current year values are unaudited.
3. The changes in the median values of ratios 1-3 for firms in the client's industry—i.e., the changes in the median from the prior

FIGURE 6

ILLUSTRATIVE OUTPUT
ACCOUNT BALANCES AND RATIOS

MONTH NO. 4 PROBLEM 1
AUDIT YEAR 19A4
IN THOUSANDS OF DOLLARS
(SOURCE : AUDIT WORKPAPERS AND CLIENT BOOKS)

ACCOUNT MONTH	19A3 (AUDITED) 4	19A4 (UNAUDITED) 3	19A4 (UNAUDITED) 4
CASH	142.	259.	169.
ACCTS REC	4629.	5505.	5337.
INVENTORY	1521.	1505.	1515.
ACCTS PAY	2817.	3311.	2961.
SALES	1667.	1947.	1660.
COST OF SALES	1233.	1467.	1108.
NET INC BT	101.	74.	174.
TOTAL ASSETS	7393.	7936.	7736.
MATERIALITY =			109.

MONTH NO. 4 PROBLEM 1
AUDIT YEAR 19A4

RATIOS

(SOURCE : AUDIT WORKPAPERS, CLIENT BOOKS AND INDUSTRY MEDIANS)

RATIO MONTH	19A3 (AUDITED) 4	19A4 (UNAUDITED) 3	19A4 (UNAUDITED) 4
1.SALES/AR (19A3 AVE= .345) (S D= .026)	.3600	.3538	.3110
2.C.S./INV (19A3 AVE= .708)* (S D= .113)	.8107	.9745	.7315
3.C.S./S (19A3 AVE= .724) (S D= .020)	.7398	.7533	.6677
4.AR/AP (19A3 AVE=1.588) (S D= .090)	1.6437	1.6628	1.8026

*ADD .10 FROM 19A3 TO 19A4 TO ADJUST FOR CHANGE IN INDUSTRY MEDIAN FOR C.S./INV

--- END OF PROBLEM 1 ---

year to the current year. CAARS uses this information to adjust its computation of the expected value for the corresponding ratio. (The Accruals Ratio is not included since this ratio is not typically tabulated by information services.)

4. The magnitude of error considered to be material for the financial statements of the current year.
5. Plots of the book values for each of the four ratios for each month of the year under audit and the audited values for the previous year.

For the recent past, audited values of the example firm's ratios have moved in about the same fashion as the median of the industry and seem to cluster around a long-run average ratio. In the absence of significant changes for the industry, upward changes in each ratio typically have been followed by downward changes of approximately the same magnitude. Furthermore, there has been little seasonal pattern to the ratios and they seem to follow a distribution that is approximately normal. This "mean reverting" pattern of ratios is typical of the ratios of many business firms even though the account balances are rising. A reasonable expectation for the value of a ratio for this firm in month t is the average audited value of the same ratio for the previous audit year adjusted for significant changes in the industry median ratio.

The standard deviation estimates give an indication of the usual range of values around the mean. Assuming that your expectation for a ratio is reasonable, the standard deviation estimate provides a measure of "reasonable" deviations from expectation.

A brief analysis follows to facilitate your understanding of the example output data in Figures 6 and 7. The data in Figure 6 are for month 4 or April of 19A4. The March and April 19A4 account balances (top half of Figure 6) and ratios (bottom half of Figure 6) for the example client are unaudited. Thus, they may be materially in error. The April 19A3 ratios and the mean of the 19A3 ratios are, however, based on audited amounts; hence, they ordinarily should *not* be interpreted as potentially in error. All account balances as well as material error are expressed in thousands of dollars; thus, materiality for the 19A4 financial statements of the firm (middle of Figure 6) is $109,000.

Figure 7 plots the values for the cost of sales to sales ratio based on audited values for 19A3 and book values for 19A4. The numerical values plotted (i.e., 3) indicate the book values of ratio number 3 for 19A4 and the "*" indicates the audited values of ratio 3 for the

FIGURE 7

ILLUSTRATIVE OUTPUT
COST OF SALES RATIO

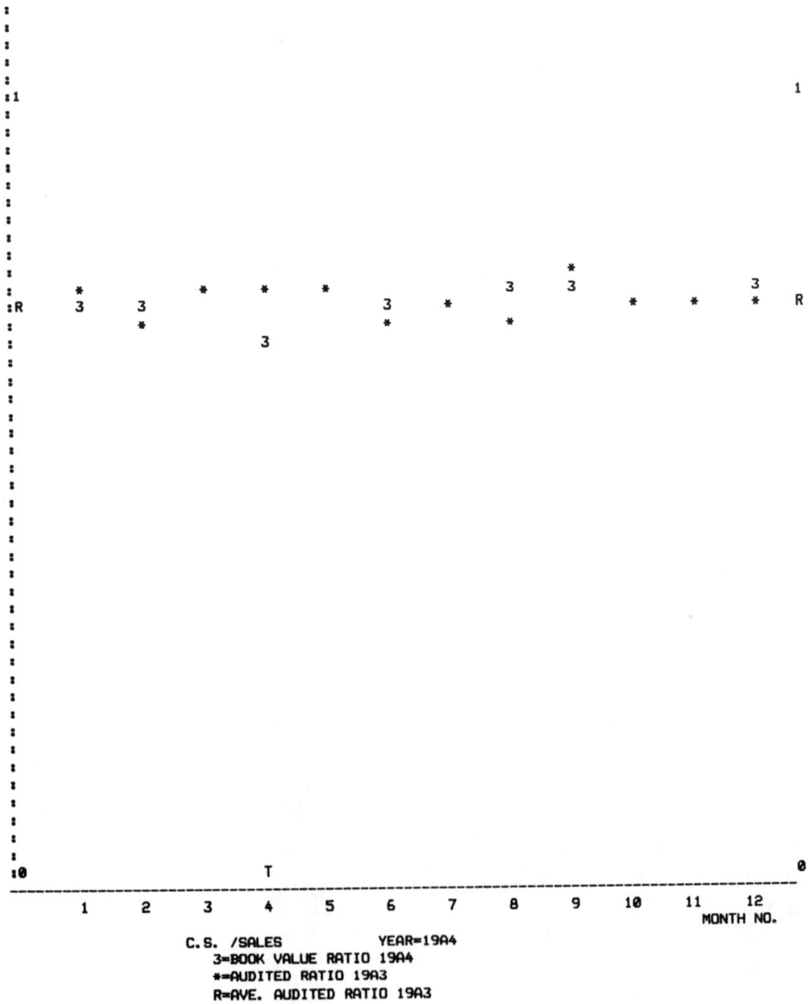

previous audit year (or if there is only a "*", that the ratio is approximately unchanged). The "R" at the left and right sides locates the 19A3 mean value of the ratio. Purchases of a material amount have been omitted during month 4 (the test month is denoted by a "T" at the bottom of the plot).

Determining which, if any, account balances or ratios are "unreasonable" based upon a subjective comparison with prior years on an account-by-account or ratio-by-ratio basis is difficult. Contrary to what you might expect, seeding an error that by itself or "individually" (see *SAS No. 47,* par. 4) equals an amount material to the *annual statements* does not, in most cases, change the value of the account balance or ratio sufficiently to be easily detected. This follows from the fact that the amount considered material is often quite small relative to a particular account balance. Recall that the amount considered material for your client is only about .5 percent of annual sales. The effect of an error of a material amount is especially small when annual balances are used. For example, if the 19A4 material amount ($109) is subtracted from the 19A4 Cost of Sales and the December 31, 19A4 Accounts Payable, the Inventory Turnover ratio changes from 8.063 to 8.009 and the Cost of Sales ratio changes from .753 to .748. Subtraction of $218 or two times the material amount changes the ratios to 7.956 and .743, or less than 1½ percent each. Random variation in annual ratios thus hides material error.

If material error is concentrated in a single month and the analysis is conducted by month as it is in this module, the error is more likely to be noticed, of course. Errors of, say, one-quarter annual materiality in each of the four months will be harder to detect in each month. However, the auditor will also have four chances to detect the error, and detection of some error in one month may lead the auditor to suspect and detect it in other months. For example, the effects of a programming error or results of a weak internal control system may be corrected in all months even though the error was indicated only in one. Strategies for detecting error spread over several months will be considered in the Regression Analysis Module.

Because of the difficulty in detecting errors in individual accounts, auditors often look for *patterns* in related accounts or ratios or the same ratio over time that are consistent with a particular type of error. For example, omitted purchases of items for resale would cause decreases in the Inventory Turnover and Cost of Sales Ratio, but would increase the Accruals Ratio. Such a pattern of changes is exhibited by these ratios for the example firm (compare 19A3 audited and 19A4 unaudited values for month 4 in Figure 6).

In the April 19A4 example, you would be correct in concluding that material purchases on account have not been recorded, thus understating cost of sales and accounts payable but overstating NIBT. We do not mean to suggest that analysis of patterns will always correctly identify the presence of material error. Such an approach does, however, seem to be a reasonable first step. The development of optimal techniques for detecting patterns in changes over time or across ratios is a valid area for research. In the exercises we will consider only a few relatively simple rules. You should recognize, however, that objective rules based on more complex patterns of monthly "cross-sections" as well as patterns of "leads and lags" may be much more effective in locating material errors.

-----You are now ready to solve problem 1-----

Problem 1

Run RATIO, problem 1. The last four (right-most) digits of your social security number will select an audit year and a particular test month. CAARS will print the client data described above, including scatter plots if you wish. Remember that you are searching for errors that overstate NIBT.

Based on the audited and book values printed out, do the following:

(a) Identify which of your client's balances and ratios, if any, appear unreasonable, i.e., appear to contain error that materially overstates NIBT. Explain the reasons for your choices.

(b) Assess which of the error conditions (omitted purchases or fictitious sales), if either, is more likely to be present. Explain how you reached your conclusion.

In problem 2 you may utilize a simple *ad hoc* rule or a univariate statistical rule. You may select one or more investigation strategies or rules (as determined by your instructor)[1] from the options available. You must also specify the magnitude of the critical value for each ratio that will trigger an analytical investigation. CAARS will compute a test statistic (described below) for each ratio which it will compare with the

[1] You can select only one rule and set of critical values at a time. Hence, if your instructor wants you to evaluate two or more rules or critical values, you must execute the program once for each combination selected.

corresponding critical value for each ratio. CAARS will signal that a particular ratio should be investigated if the test statistic for that ratio is more extreme than your critical value in the direction of the predicted change in the ratio for each error (see Figure 4). In other words, CAARS will indicate that the Accounts Receivable Turnover Ratio and the Accruals ratio should be investigated if their test statistics are greater than the corresponding critical values specified by you. For the Inventory Turnover and Cost of Sales ratios, CAARS will signal an investigation if their test statistics are less than your critical values. Thus CAARS relieves you of all the computations so that you can focus your attention on specifying the critical value for each ratio. To give you a basis from which to start thinking about your choice of investigation rule and critical values, the same error condition that was present in problem 1 will also be present in problems 2 and 3. Consequently, you should use the knowledge gained in problem 1 in selecting your rule(s) and in specifying your critical value(s) for problems 2 and 3.

Ad hoc Rule (Rule 1)

For the *ad hoc* rule, the critical value you must specify is a percentage change in the value of a ratio. A single prior month could be the basis of comparison with the test month. For example, if your test month is February of 19A4, the basis for comparison could be February 19A3. However, since there is little seasonal variation, we use the prior year's mean adjusted for any significant changes in the industry median as the expected ratio. This is done to average out random fluctuations in the audited values for particular months.

The deviation is computed as follows:

Test Statistic: $\frac{r_t - \hat{r}_t}{r_t}$

where:

r_t = the book value of a ratio in month t of the current (audit) period, and

$\hat{r}_t$ = the expected audited value of a ratio for t, or in this problem, the audited value of r for the previous audit year adjusted for significant change in the industry median.[2]

Decision rule: Investigate accounts comprising r_t if the calculated test statistic is more extreme than your preset "critical value" for the deviation.

[2] Keep in mind the fact that $\bar{r}$ as adjusted is assumed to be the expected value of r_t ($E(r_t)$) for the test company for this time period. For other companies or for this company for other periods, a more complicated expectations model may be appropriate.

Critical Percentages for Rule 1: You must choose critical values for the magnitude of the percentage change that will trigger an investigation. The value may vary from ratio to ratio based on how much a material error might affect the ratio. The smaller the critical percentage, e.g., two percent, the more likely the calculated test statistic will exceed the critical percentage; hence, the more frequently an investigation will be signaled. The danger, therefore, in choosing small critical values is that they can lead to an excessive frequency of type I errors (no error, but investigate). Conversely, the larger the critical percentage, e.g., 20 percent, the less likely it is that the calculated test statistic will exceed the critical percentage and the less frequently an error will be signaled. The danger, therefore, in choosing large critical values is that they can lead to an excessive frequency of type II errors (error but no investigation). The larger the monetary error actually present in the accounts, the better the rules will work, i.e., the fewer type I or type II errors they will make. The most difficult (material) monetary error to detect will be one that is just equal to a material amount.

Univariate Statistical Rule (Rule 2)

Univariate statistical rules utilize the probability distribution of monthly audited values of each ratio for your client firm. The rule here uses the standard deviation of the 12 monthly ratios for the previous audit year. The rule triggers an investigation when the difference between the client's recorded values for the test month and the expected ratio is so large in relation to past differences in the ratio that it is unlikely that the difference can be attributed to chance. You investigate because it may be due to error.

Let s_r denote the standard deviation of the previous year's audited values of r (s_r is also an estimate of the standard deviation of audited values for the audit year). A 1-α one-sided confidence limit on r can be calculated by considering an allowance for random factor effects based on s_r. For example, the upper confidence limit is $\hat{r}_t + Z_{1-\alpha}(s_r)$ or the lower confidence limit is $\hat{r}_t - Z_{1-\alpha}(s_r)$.[3] An investigation is indicated if r_t lies beyond the applicable limit.

An equivalent calculation and decision rule is to "standardize" r_t by subtracting $\hat{r}_t$ and dividing the difference by s_r. This expression of the test statistic in standard deviation units allows the use of a standard normal "Z" table. Thus:

---

[3] For simplicity, we use standard normal "Z" values instead of "t."

Test Statistic: $\frac{r_t - \hat{r}_t}{s_r}$ or $\frac{\Delta r}{s_r}$

Decision rule: Investigate accounts comprising r_t if the calculated test statistic is more extreme than the critical "Z" value for the deviation.

An investigation is indicated whenever the test statistic is greater than (less than) the critical normal deviate "Z" value you specify. CAARS will signal an investigation is needed if $\Delta r/s_r > Z_{1-\alpha}$ (or $\Delta r/s_r < -Z_{1-\alpha}$ depending on the ratio). Corresponding to any Z value you specify is an alpha value (α) representing the probability that the change in your clients' ratio ($\Delta r/s_r$) at least as large (small) as the Z value you specified could have occurred by chance, i.e., in the absence of accounting error.

To illustrate, suppose that after evaluating the costs of a type I and a type II error, you decide that a type I error rate of .333 is reasonable for the investigation of the Accounts Receivable Turnover ratio. That is, when no accounting error is present, you are willing to investigate a seemingly large increase in the ratio about one-third of the time. You use the expectation and the historical standard deviation estimate to calculate an upper confidence limit on the audited value of the ratio. The normal deviate "Z" value to yield 33 percent of the area in the right tail of a normal distribution is .44. Thus, for our illustration of April 19A4, CAARS will compute the test statistic as (.311 − .345)/.026 or −1.308. CAARS will signal an investigation of the possibility of material overstatement of earnings if the test statistic is greater than .44. In other words, if the standardized change in the ratio is greater than .44, the auditor will conclude that the fluctuation is too large to be due to chance and may well be due to an error such as the entry of fictitious credit sales. In our April 19A4 example, CAARS does not indicate that these accounts need more than ordinary audit attention.

Note that the test statistics for rule 1 and rule 2 have the same numerator. The denominator for rule 2 requires that the auditor calculate s_r but it offers the advantage of being "self-scaling." That is, a .44 value for Z will yield one-third in a tail for any normal distribution whether the usual changes are large or small in relation to the expected ratio. Rule 1 requires that the auditor "scale" the investigation probabilities by the choice of different critical values for ratios with different variabilities.

Critical "Z" Values for Rule 2: In choosing the value of $Z_{1-\alpha}$ to be compared with the test statistic to determine whether to investigate, you are implicitly setting the type I error risk of a "false" investigation (i.e., α). The usual sequence, of course, is to choose the risk level and then determine the appropriate Z value. Some commonly selected values of α and the corresponding "critical" $Z_{1-\alpha}$ values are:

To yield type I error risk (α) of	you should set $Z_{1-\alpha}$ equal to
.10	1.28
.20	.85
.30	.53
.33	.44
.40,	.26.

Note that the smaller the α chosen, the larger the $Z_{1-\alpha}$. This implies that the smaller the α you choose, the less likely it is that an investigation will be indicated. Therefore, the smaller the value of α, the greater the likelihood of a type II error (error but no investigation). Conversely, larger values of α yield smaller $Z_{1-\alpha}$ and lesser likelihood of a type II error. In fact, the value of α is the probability of a type I error (no error, but investigate) under the condition of no accounting error if your expectations model for $\hat{r}_t$ is reasonable, s_r is accurate, and the distribution of ratios is normal. Like the percentage change rules, the effectiveness of this univariate statistical rule in controlling type II error will vary with the relative size of the actual monetary error in the account balances. (Remember that when executing rule 2, you are to specify the $Z_{1-\alpha}$ value rather than α itself.)

Pattern Analysis

The output for problems 2, 3, and 4 includes a crude ratio deviation "pattern analysis" for the monthly cross-sections of the first three ratios. Specifically, CAARS compares the combination of signals to investigate for Accounts Receivable Turnover, Inventory Turnover, and the Cost of Sales Ratio with the combination to be expected if either of the two specified types of error is present. This comparison is based on the direction analysis shown in Figure 4. The Accruals Ratio is not included since it, like the Cost of Sales Ratio, changes in the same direction for both errors, but the Accruals Ratio seems to be less diagnostic than the Cost of Sales Ratio.

If both Accounts Receivable Turnover and the Cost of Sales Ratio indicate that an investigation is needed, CAARS will write a message to be alert for possibly material fictitious credit sales. Similarly, if both Inventory Turnover and the Cost of Sales Ratio indicate an investigation, the message is to be alert for omitted credit purchases. If both turnover ratios or all three ratios signal an investigation, then the pattern message indicates an alert for either or both errors. Finally, if fewer than two ratios indicate an investigation, there is no alert for either error.

It should be noted that the pattern analysis is based on a search for patterns related to two particular types of errors. Thus, while the analysis seems to be potentially useful, it requires an analysis of how various errors would be reflected in the accounts. There are, of course, many possible types of accounting errors. To use the pattern analysis approach, some thought must be given to a "menu" of possible errors (e.g., see Coakley and Loebbecke [1985] and *SAS No. 1,* section 320.62) and an analysis of how the accounts would be affected by each error on the menu. The development of such analyses is a topic for further study. Our purpose in this exercise is to become exposed to some of the possibilities.

----You are now ready to solve problem 2----

Problem 2

Problem 2 asks you to analyze your client's ratios for a particular month of the year under audit using one of the investigation rules described above. Once you have selected an investigation rule and specified the critical values for each ratio (you may choose a different value for each ratio), the program will compute the investigation decision for each ratio and indicate whether that decision was, in fact, correct (CDI = correct decision to investigate; CDO = correct decision not to investigate) or in error (TI = type I error; TII = type II error). Whenever the value of the test statistic (TEST) exceeds the specified critical value (CRIT), an investigation is signaled. You should compare the result you obtain here with your subjective investigation decisions in problem 1.

When you have studied your own output for problem 2, answer the following questions.

(a) What error is seeded? Which accounts are affected?
(b) Which ratios give the correct investigation signals?
(c) Compare your subjective evaluation from problem 1 with the

results of your rule for problem 2. Are you surprised? Briefly explain.

(d) If you used rule 2, the graph in your output shows the standard normal (Z) distribution and standardized deviations in the ratio (i.e., $\Delta r/s_r$). Do you see a pattern in the fluctuations that suggests the type of error that was present? What does your answer imply concerning the magnitude of a material error relative to normal variation in the ratio?

Phase II—Analysis of All 48 Months

In this phase of the Financial Ratio Analysis Module, we repeat the financial ratio analysis of problem 2 but add the other 11 months of your test year as well as the other three audit years. In problem 3 the same error as was seeded in problems 1 and 2 is used. The objective is to give you some perspective on the overall effectiveness of your investigation rule and critical values as economic conditions may change over time.

Each error is seeded and the program run independently in each of the analyses. That is, the other 11 months of the audit year and the 12 months of the previous audit year do not have accounting error added. Also, it should be noted that the months after the "test" month *are not* considered by the computer analysis—it is based on the test month alone.

Thus, the analysis in problem 3 consists of 48 replications (one for each month) of the analysis in problem 2 using the rule and critical values you specify. The results of this analysis are tabulated by ratio to indicate the total number of type I errors (TI), type II errors (TII), correct decisions not to investigate (CDO), and correct decisions to investigate (CDI) for the 48-month period. The type I and type II errors for each ratio are also tabulated by month and by year.

The output for problems 3 and 4 includes a summary of the "pattern analysis" messages over the 48-month sample period. Thus, one can assess the investigation error rates for the pattern analysis approach. Specifically, one can see the number of correct signals to investigate the error that was, in fact, seeded as compared to the number of signals to investigate with no indication of the type of error, the signals to investigate the wrong error, or signals to investigate when no error was present.

----You are now ready to solve Problem 3----

Problem 3

After studying your own output for problem 3, answer the following questions.

(a) Which ratio gave the "best" or most diagnostic investigation signals?
(b) Evaluate how well your rule and critical value performed over the 48 cases. Are you satisfied? How would you change your choices?
(c) Did your rule and critical value perform particularly well for certain calendar months or years? Why might this be?
(d) Try a second rule or critical value. (For example, if you believe that the type II error rate for a particular ratio is too high, you might lower the absolute magnitude of the critical value.) Which seems to perform better? How do you explain this superiority?

In problem 4 there are three replications of all 48 months with three error conditions seeded. Specifically, you receive a 48-month analysis of the problem with no accounting error seeded and analyses with each of the two types of errors seeded each month. The objective is to see how a rule performs over each type of error and with no added error.

In problem 4, the rule and critical values you specify are applied for each of the error conditions (no error, omitted purchases, and fictitious sales) for the 48 months. Thus, problem 4 consists of three replications of the analysis in problem 3, one for each error condition. This should give you additional perspective on the effectiveness of your investigation rule and critical values over various error conditions. The results of this analysis are tabulated by ratio as in problem 3.

----You are now ready to solve Problem 4----

Problem 4

After you have studied your output for each type of error as well as the no-error condition, answer the following questions:

(a) Did any one ratio consistently give the best signals for all types of error?
(b) Evaluate how well your rule and critical value performed over the 48 cases with each error type.

(c) Try a second rule or critical value. Which seems to perform better? How do you explain this superiority?

(d) In general, how effective do you think ratio analysis is as an audit tool for signalling individually material accounting errors? Is it cost-effective?

(e) (Optional) CAARS will allow you to experiment with different amounts of error (see Authors' Note below). Enter "9" as the problem number to get the menu to change the materiality seeding factor, then run problem 4 again. How does your answer to question 4 above change when the amount of error seeded is 2.0 × materiality or .5 × materiality? What implications does your answer have for reliance on ratio analysis as an attention director and as a test of details substitute?

Phase III—Tentative Explanation Analysis

A potential problem with analytical review procedures as an attention director or as a substitute for tests of details is the risk that the auditor will stop the analytical investigation of an unusual fluctuation before its actual cause has been found. That is, the auditor may prematurely terminate or "truncate" the investigation of fluctuations that have been identified in the initial stage of analytical review.

An auditor is under time pressure to obtain sufficient competent audit evidence and complete the examination as soon as possible. Therefore, the auditor may accept a seemingly plausible explanation without adequate analysis of all of its implications. A "truncated analytical investigation" is potentially important since the auditor may not have sufficiently investigated a problem or may restrict other substantive tests in reliance on the seemingly satisfactory analytical review results.

One way to guard against the problem of truncated analytical investigation is to work through the implications of a proposed or tentative explanation of an unusual fluctuation. Specifically, the auditor can make an "as-if" entry to reverse the effect of the tentative explanation as if it were, in fact, correct. The auditor then conducts an analytical review of the tentatively revised numbers.

If the tentative explanation is correct, then the revised analysis should yield fewer exceptions or unusual fluctations than did the analysis using book values. On the other hand, if the explanation is incorrect, the revised ratios are likely to exhibit even more unusual relationships than before. That is, while an explanation is likely to account for at least some of the fluctuations, an incorrect explanation will add to or subtract from accounts that were not in error or may add (subtract) an amount when, in fact, an error already exists.

To see how and why the tentative explanation analysis might work, consider a situation in which cost of sales is unusually small and therefore the cost of sales to sales ratio is smaller than expected. Cost of sales might be small due to:

a) an omitted purchase,
b) overcounting the ending inventory,
c) overpricing the ending inventory,
d) cost reductions due to a new economic-order quantity model or
e) a shift in product mix to goods with an unusually high contribution margin.

The other side of the cost of sales entries implied by these explanations is quite different. For example, a) and perhaps d) involve payables, while only e) involves sales and the others involve ending inventory. Also note that d) and e) involve normal business activities and not errors. One might expect that d) and e) would be offered by management and its employees as explanations for a decrease in the Cost of Sales Ratio. If management's explanation is, in fact, correct, then a ratio analysis based on the tentatively revised numbers should produce fewer unusual fluctuations.

Figure 7 shows example output for April 19A4, based on Problem 5. It shows standardized values ($\Delta r/s_r$) of the four ratios for your test month, along with a plot of a standard normal distribution and integer values of the standard deviation for reference. Credit purchases of a material amount have been omitted, and thus materially understate cost of sales and accounts payable. For almost all of the possible test months, the Cost of Sales Ratio is several standard deviations below its expectation and is a likely candidate for an analytical investigation.

We would expect that an adjustment based on the correct explanation of an omitted purchase would bring the cost of sales ratio as well as the other ratios affected by this error closer to their respective expected values. However, an adjustment based on an incorrect explanation will introduce more error and will probably move some of the other ratios further from their expected values.

Panel (1) of Figure 8 shows a plot of ratios based on the book values (with omitted purchases). Panel (2) shows the book values adjusted for the controller's incorrect explanation. Notice that while ratio 3 (the Cost of Sales Ratio) is closer to its expected value of zero,

FIGURE 8

TENTATIVE EXPLANATION ANALYSIS

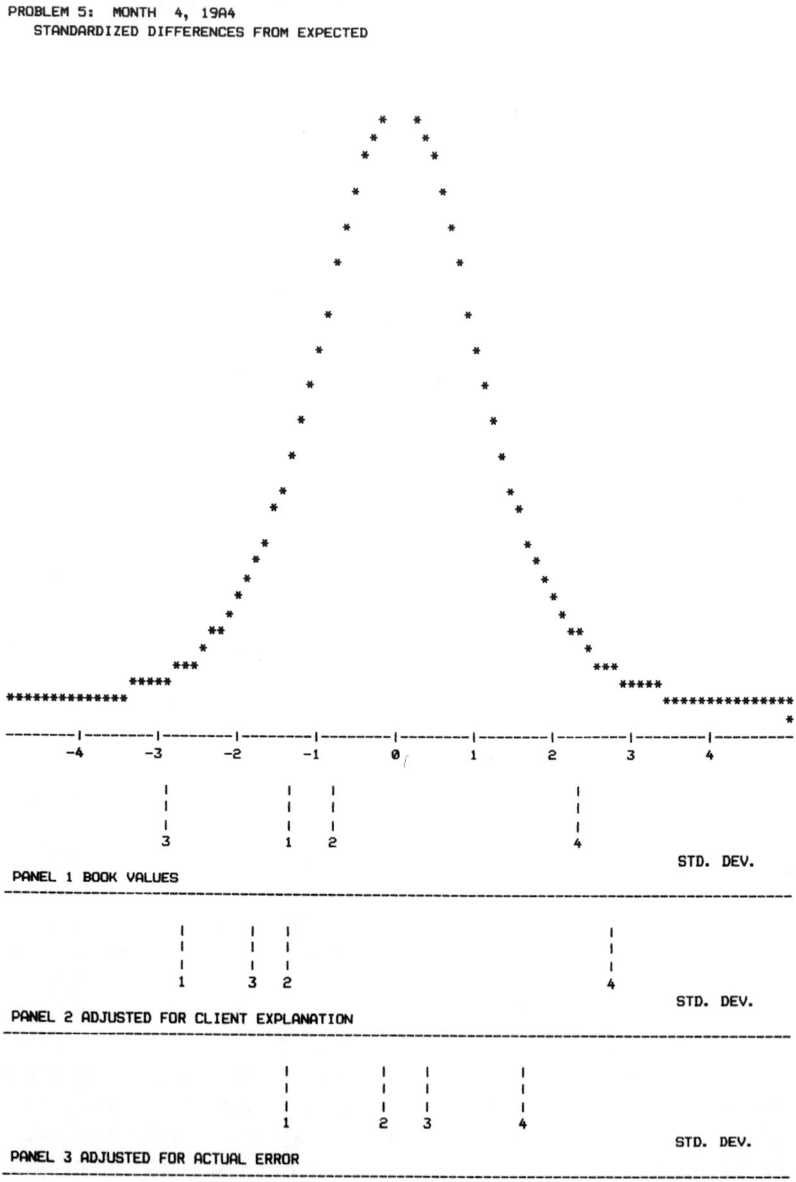

the other three ratios are *further* from zero. Panel (3) shows the ratios with the correct explanation (i.e., the audited amounts). For the correct explanation, all three of the affected ratios are closer to zero.

The "tentative explanation analysis" as discussed above will not always be effective, of course. Some explanations have patterns of contra-entries that are very similar to those of other explanations. However, the revised ratio analysis will guard against accepting some explanations and is very cheap to apply when a computer-assisted system is being used.

----You are now ready to solve Problem 5----

Problem 5

Problem 5 allows you to test the sensitivity of financial ratio analysis to alternative explanations of possible causes. In this problem an error that materially overstates gross profit and NIBT has been seeded—specifically, material purchases for resale have not been recorded for your test month. Therefore, you are very likely to get a signal to investigate the reduction in the cost of sales ratio for your test month.

As part of your analytical investigation of the fluctuation, you make inquiry of the client's controller. She suggests that the reduction in the Cost of Sales Ratio is probably due to acquisition and sale of a special line of books for the test month. The special line cost the client $98,000 and was sold during the test month at a markup of 100 percent. You decide to follow up on this suggested explanation by conducting a tentative explanation analysis. To do this, you "back out" the entries that would have been due to the special acquisition and sale. Specifically, you subtract $196,000 from sales and subtract $98,000 from cost of sales and NIBT. At month end you assume that three-quarters of these special sales had been collected but none of the liability had been paid, and your "adjustments" to receivables and payables reflect these assumptions.

The computer output for problem 5 is a standardized ratio analysis. Panel (1) shows results using the client's book values. This is the analysis that led to your investigation of the test month. Panel (2) shows the ratios after adjustment for the controller's explanation and panel (3) shows the ratios after correction of the actual error that had been seeded.

(a) Compare panel (2) with panel (1). Does the controller's suggestion appear to explain the fluctuation? Why or why not?
(b) Compare panel (3) with panel (1). Does the pattern in panel (3) seem to be more consistent with a "zero accounting error" pattern? Is the comparison consistent with the error that was, in fact, seeded? Explain your reasoning.
(c) Given your analysis, how might you follow up your analytical investigation? That is, what subsequent tests or inquiries about the accounts or internal accounting controls might be appropriate?

---Authors' Note---

If you wish to change the parameters or the error seeding of problems 1-4 (problem 5 can't be altered), enter "9" when the program asks you to select a problem number. After you specify the month, year (19A2 = 2, etc.), error seeding amount (in materiality units), and error type (0 = no error, 1 = omitted purchases, 2 = fictitious sales), you will again be asked to enter a problem number (1-4). Since problems 3 and 4 use all months and years, your month and year selections will be ignored if you run problem 3 or 4. Similarly, problem 4 will ignore your error type selection since it uses both error types as well as the no error. (If you specify no error, the error amount seeding factor will be ignored.)

Your selections will remain in place for the next problem run. If you want to run several problems or one problem more than once, you will have to first run problem 9 and enter your changes each time.

Three

Regression Analysis Module

Introduction

There are several different ways that the multivariate statistical approach using regression analysis can be applied in the context of an auditor's analytical review of a client's balance sheet or income statement accounts.[1] For example, regression analysis can be used to find the relationship among or between variables measured at a common point in time (a cross-sectional regression) or to find a relationship measured over several periods of time (a time-series regression). Because it has wider application and is somewhat easier to apply, the analyses in this booklet will concentrate on the use of a time-series regression in the analytical review of an income statement account. The major points learned from a study of time-series are also relevant to understanding cross-sectional applications.

To begin, consider the time-series of monthly balances of an income statement account. Let y_t ($t = 1, 2, \ldots, m$) denote the audited value of a particular month t of that series. For example, y_t might be sales for the client firm for month t. The auditor must express an opinion as to the fairness of the sum of the 12 as yet unaudited counterparts of y_t for the year under audit (i.e., $t = m + 1, \ldots, m + 12$). Assume an ideal situation in which y_t in the base or prior-to-current-audit period ($t = 1$ to m) and in the audit period ($t = m + 1$ to $m + 12$) is linearly related to an independent variable series, series x_t. The x_t value might be an index of sales for firms in the client's industry. The relationship is:

$$y_t = A + Bx_t = e_t \qquad \text{(equation 1)}$$

where A and B are the regression coefficients that express the "average" or usual relationship of an x_t to y_t, and e_t is a residual or

[1] This discussion draws heavily from Kinney and Salamon [1982].

unexplained part of y_t. The e_t series is normally and identically distributed with mean zero and standard deviation S. In the real world these assumptions about e_t will not be met exactly. However, there are many situations in which they are close enough to be useful.

Under these conditions the auditor can estimate A, B, and S using ordinary least-squares regression. Let a, b, and s denote the ordinary least-squares estimates. Assuming that x_t is available for 12 months of the audit year (t = m + 1 through m + 12), the auditor can then compute the conditional expectation of y_t given x_t (denoted $\hat{y}_t$) via

$$\hat{y}_t = a + bx_t. \qquad \text{(equation 2)}$$

The residual term in equation 2 is zero since the expectation of e_t for any month t is zero. Given our assumptions, the $\hat{y}_t$ is an unbiased, minimum variance estimate of the *audited value* for the account in month t. Under these conditions, regression analysis allows the auditor to evaluate the statistical significance of the difference between the client recorded values (denoted y_{rt}) and the expected audited values ($\hat{y}_t$) for the year as a whole or on a month-by-month basis. The exact procedures for determining the statistical significance of these differences are described below.

In concept, the investigation decision for the multivariate statistical method is much like the univariate investigation decision. The auditor decides to investigate when the book value appears to be unreasonable given his or her prior knowledge as measured by the statistical confidence interval. The analysis is complicated by the addition of the x variable(s). However, the "information" in x may allow more precise expectations of y.

To illustrate for a single month, assume that the auditor has obtained a, b, and s from a regression analysis based on x_t and audited y_t for a 36-month "base" period (months 1-36). The value of x is available for month 37 but y_{r37} is as yet unaudited. The auditor can calculate the estimated audited value ($\hat{y}_{37}$) via

$$\hat{y}_{37} = a + bx_{37}$$

This provides an unbiased point estimate of audited value for month 37 given the current x_{37} under the past relationship between y_t and x_t. If there is no accounting error in y_{r37}, about half the time the point estimate will be under the actual audited value and about half the time the estimate will be over. How much under or over it is likely to be depends, in part, on s.

The auditor can use s from the base period regression to calculate the standard error of prediction of y_{37}—denoted s_{37}. The s_{37} is an allowance for random variation or error in the estimates. Then, using "t" table values and $\hat{y}_{37}$, the upper or lower confidence limit on $\hat{y}_{37}$ can be determined. For example, to obtain the .80 upper limit, the "t" value would be approximately .852. The .80 upper confidence limit (UCL) on $\hat{y}_{37}$ would be

$$UCL_{.8}\ (y_{37}) = a + bx_{37} + .852s_{37}$$

The interpretation of $UCL_{.8}\ (y_{37})$ is that, under the past relationship between y_t and x_t and the current x_{37}, 80 percent of the audited values of the account in a month with the independent variable x taking on the value x_{37} would fall below $UCL_{.8}\ (y_{37})$. If y_{r37} is greater than $UCL_{.8}\ (y_{37})$, the auditor might decide to investigate since its value seems likely to be overstated.

To relate the upper confidence limit calculation to "materiality" or the "tolerable error" for an account, many auditors find it useful to subtract audited value estimates from the known book value to get a UCL on *monetary error*. That is, for our example month 37, they would calculate $\hat{e}_{37} = y_{r37} - \hat{y}_{37}$ and

$$UCL_{.8}\ (e_{37}) = \hat{e}_{37} + \text{"t"}_{.8,34}\ s_{37}.$$

The UCL on error provides an estimate of "how large the error might be after allowing for random error variation in our estimates." If UCL on error exceeds the amount deemed reasonable or "tolerable" for the month, then the auditor would investigate to determine whether the balance may, indeed, be "intolerably" overstated due to accounting error. The investigation is conducted since the auditor is less than 80 percent confident that the recorded value y_{r37} is not "intolerably" overstated.

Statistical inferences about the validity of recorded values depend upon the assumption that the simple regression model is an appropriate expression of the relationship betweeen y_t and x_t. If, in a particular audit engagement, the assumptions for the regression model do not seem to hold, then the model *cannot* be relied upon by the auditor to produce statistically valid inferences about the client's recorded values. Therefore, a critical part of any attempt to use regression in analytical review is to assess whether the assumptions associated with the regression model are met or can be met with simple data transformation. A complete discussion of this issue is, of course, beyond the scope of this booklet.[2] However, we do present a brief discussion of those assumptions and how various data plots may be used as guides for determining whether the assumptions are met in a particular application.

Regression Model Assumptions

In equation (1) the assumptions of the regression model are stated or implied. Equation (1) suggests that y_t has two components: a systematic or explained component $(A + Bx_t)$ and a residual or unexplained component (e_t). Notice that the unkown parameters (A,B) in the systematic component of the relationship between y_t and x_t do not have a t subscript. This means that we are assuming that the true intercept and slope parameters are the same in all months included in the analysis $(t = 1 \text{ to } m + 12)$.

Beneath equation (1) it is stated that the unexplained component of the relationship between y_t and x_t (e_t) is assumed to be a random variable which is distributed NID $(0, S^2)$. This is a compact way of making several assumptions at once. First, it is assumed that the e_t are independent random variables and they all have an identical probability distribution—a normal probability distribution. The expected value or mean of *each* of these probability distributions is zero. Furthermore, the variance of each of these distributions is unknown but is assumed to be the same for each time period (as indicated again by the absence of a t subscript on S^2).

If all the assumptions of the simple regression model are approximately met in a particular application, then the model can provide the basis for statistically valid inferences in an analytical review of a client's account. In general, the way the auditor would proceed in using regression in analytical review would be to *tentatively* hypothesize that the regression model assumptions are met for the client's base or pre-audit period data, and run the simple regression in the base period (i.e., obtain the estimates of A, B, and S (a, b, and s)). Then the auditor would review the results to see if the tentative hypothesis of no assumption violations seems sensible in the case of this client's set of data. In contemporary audit practice auditors have developed computer-generated diagnostics as a part of the regression analysis computer program. Thus, many of the tests of assumptions are conducted automatically and are "invisible" to the auditor. For

[2] For further discussion and references see Kinney and Salamon [1978].

illustrative purposes we will discuss the scanning of various data plots in an attempt to discover if assumption violations appear to exist.

If the regression assumptions are not violated, then the a and b produced by ordinary least-squares regression are unbiased estimates of the unknown parameters A and B. This means that an *estimate* of the true unexplained part of y_t (which we earlier labeled e_t) can be found by

$$\hat{e}_t = y_t - (a + bx_t). \qquad \text{(equation 3)}$$

In a typical time-series application, the auditor would be interested in three data plots: (1) a plot of y_t against x_t; (2) a plot of $\hat{e}_t$ against x_t; (3) a plot of $\hat{e}_t$ against time. Figure 9 displays these three plots for a typical case in which no regression model assumptions are violated.

Figure 9, panel (1) displays the plot of y_t versus x_t. In this plot, the auditor can subjectively assess the general form and closeness of the relationship. For example, the auditor might look for any kind of curvature in the relationship between y_t and x_t. If such curvature is present, it may indicate that the relationship is not linear (i.e., the relationship could be quadratic or even a higher-order polynomial). In addition, the auditor might look for "breaks" in plot of y_t versus x_t that would indicate slope or intercept changes at a particular value of the independent variable x.

Figure 9, panel (2) displays the plot of $\hat{e}_t$ versus x_t. The $\hat{e}_t$ seem to cluster near zero for all x values. Thus, in this application the assumption of a zero mean for e_t at all x values seems to be a reasonable one. In addition, notice that the *range* of the $\hat{e}_t$ values in panel (b) of Figure 9 seems be about the same at all values of x_t. Thus, the assumption that the e_t have the same variance at all x values seems to be a reasonable one. Economic data often have a wider range of values at higher volumes of business. If this is the case, the auditor may need to transform those data before applying the regression model. One common transformation is to use the square root of y_t in place of y_t. This reduces large values of y_t by more than small values and may yield homogeneous variance at all values of x. If the $\hat{e}_t$ were mostly negative for some range of x_t and mostly positive for other ranges, then the auditor might suspect that the slope and/or intercept of the regression line is different for some values of x_t. If this were the case, "dummy" or "indicator" variables might have to be added to the regression model before the auditor could rely on its inferences.

Figure 9, panel (3) displays the plot of $\hat{e}_t$ versus time or the month number (t). This plot allows the auditor to assess the assumptions that

FIGURE 9
SCATTERPLOTS OF y_t, x_t, e_t and t
Panel 1

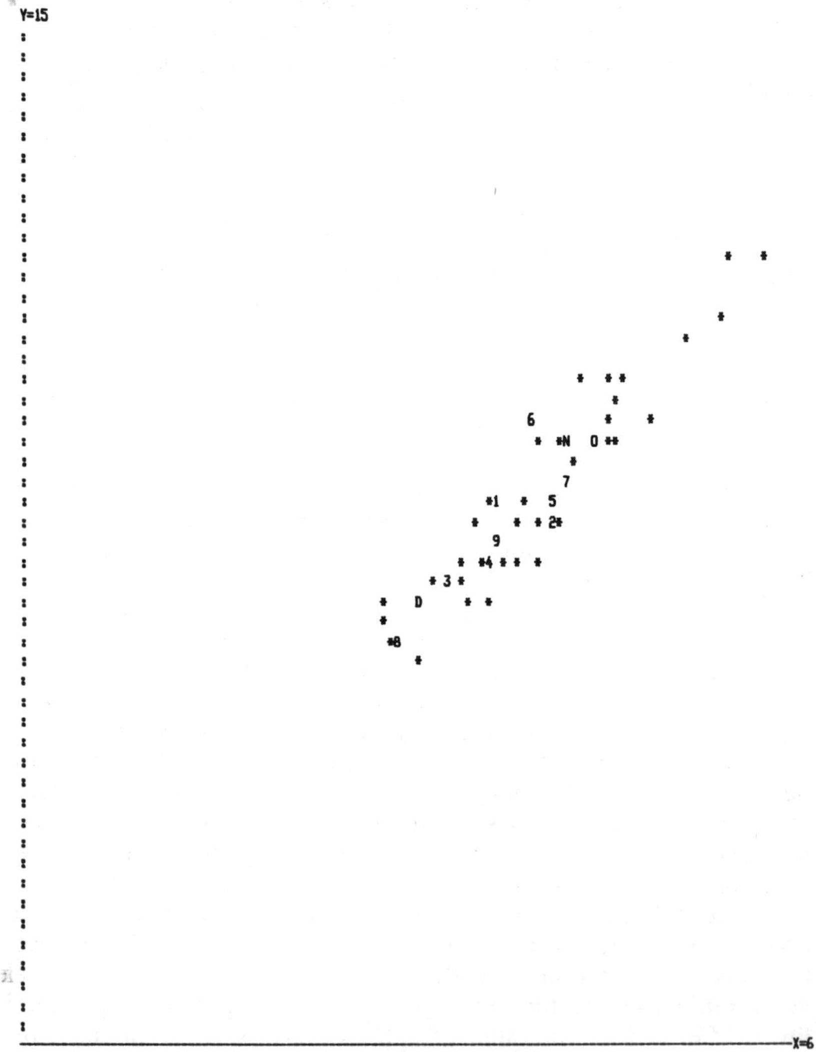

BASE PERIOD VALUES INDICATED AS *
AUDIT PERIOD VALUES INDICATED AS FOLLOWS:
JAN-SEPT INDICATED BY 1-9
OCT-DEC INDICATED BY O,N,D

FIGURE 9
Panel 2

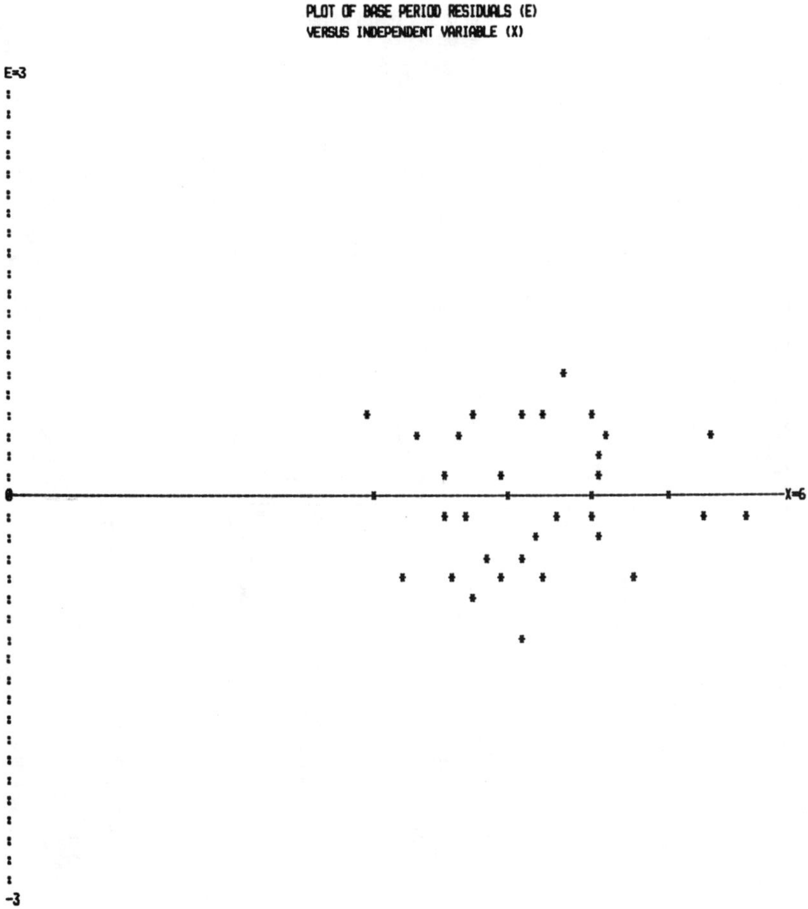

FIGURE 9
Panel 3

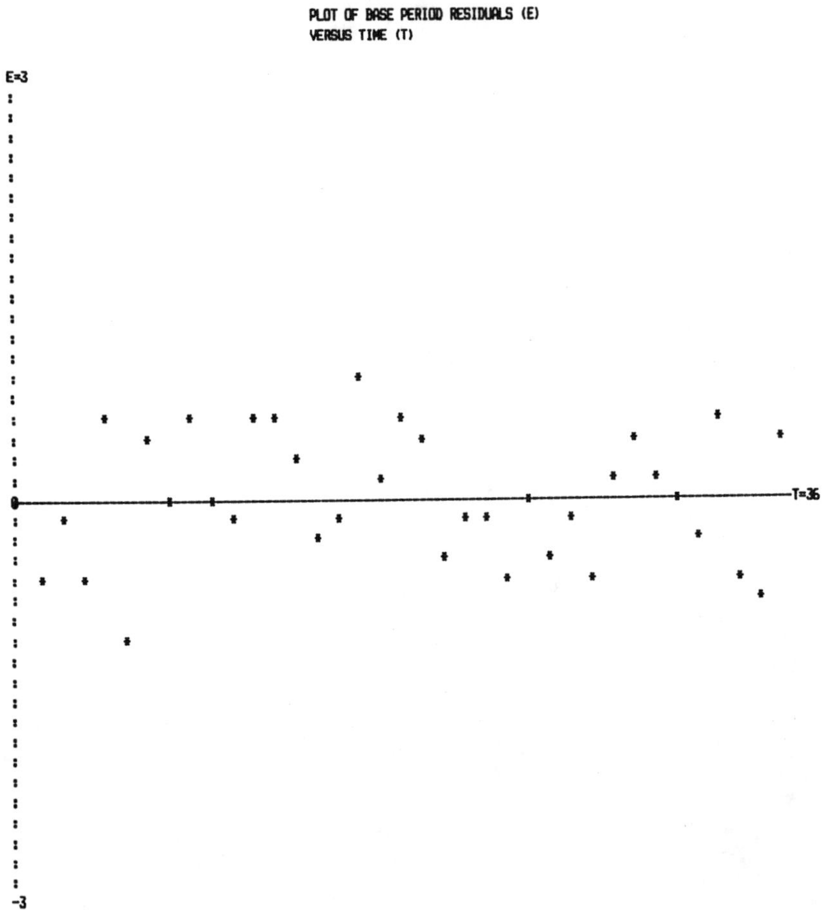

the e_t have a zero mean and constant variance over the entire base period. Also, the auditor can assess whether the slope and/or intercept may have changed over time. Here, the auditor looks for a pattern in the estimated residuals which would indicate a difference in the relationship between y_t and x_t in the early versus the late part of the base period ($t = 1$ to 36). For example, the relationship for $t = 21$ to 36 may be different from that for $t = 1$ to 20. If such a pattern in the estimated residuals existed, the auditor would have to appropriately modify the simple regression model, perhaps by including additional slope or intercept coefficients for each subperiod.

Accounting data series will often require transformation, the addition of other independent variables, or the addition of coefficients before the assumptions of regression analysis appear to be met. Regression audit software typically provides warnings of possible violations and suggests remedies. Since assumption violation is a *statistical* problem that often has an adequate solution, we will not dwell on it here. In this booklet (except for problem 2), we assume that the appropriate model validity checks (including analysis of data and residual plots) have been made and have provided no reason to suspect a violation of the assumptions of the simple regression model. You are reminded, however, that there may be no statistical validity to the procedures described if the assumptions associated with the model are seriously violated. Thus, determining model validity is a *necessary* step in the successful application of regression in the analytical review.

Using Regression in Analytical Review

The auditor must form an opinion as to the fairness of annual balances comprising financial statements. Tests of the annual balance at the desired level of confidence can be developed by focusing on the 12-month balance or each month comprising the annual balance. One large auditing firm follows the latter approach. It uses the results of a regression analysis to compute an upper confidence limit on accounting error in an account balance for each month of the audit year and compares it with a critical value for error for each month. The critical value is based on annual tolerable error and its possible distribution throughout the year. In this booklet we use regression analysis to calculate an upper confidence limit on accounting error for the entire year under audit and compare the limit with tolerable error for the year directly. We then follow up with a test for unusually large monthly residuals or "outliers." Both the overall annual balance and the monthly balance approaches use the same underlying environmental data and either can be effective at the stated risk level. We have chosen the annual balance approach with follow-up tests for monthly outliers since it is somewhat easier to understand.

In the remainder of this section, we present the specifics of how regression can be used to formulate tests for error using the annual balance method and then follow up by searching the individual monthly balances for unusual amounts.

Annual Balance Test

Conceptually, the regression-based test of an annual account balance is quite simple. First, the auditor must establish the desired risk level for type II error (the probability of not investigating an account balance containing intolerable error) for the analytical review procedure. Given this risk level (denoted β), the auditor uses information from the regression analysis to calculate an upper confidence limit for monetary error in the annual balance and compares this "upper limit" on error to the amount of error in the annual balance that is considered to be "intolerable." That is, the amount of error that, when aggregated with errors in other accounts, would lead to materially misstated financial statements (*SAS No. 39,* par. 18). Let E* denote the "intolerable" error magnitude for the annual balance of the account. If the "upper limit" on error in the annual balance is less than the intolerable amount (E*), then the auditor can conclude that the annual balance is unlikely—at the specified level of risk—to contain intolerable error.

Since particular audit procedures for tests of details are usually effective on errors of only one direction, the auditor's interests in analytical review will often be in indicating errors of one sign only. Consequently, in what follows, we will concentrate on the detection of *overstatement* errors.

The mechanics of the annual balance test require estimates of total monetary error in the account for the 12 months of the audit year ($\hat{E}$), the standard deviation of total error (s_E), and the (1-β) upper precision limit on total overstatement error ($UCL_{1-\beta}$ (E)). $\hat{E}$ is simply the book value of the account minus the sum of the monthly audited value estimates. The s_E is a standard deviation measure based on the s from the regression analysis adjusted for the fact that 12 predictions are used to estimate the audited value for the year. Finally, the UCL on total error is based on the same calculation we made in the univariate statistical method of part two of the booklet and the previous regression example of this part.

The formulas for these estimates are:

$$\hat{E} = \sum_{t=m+1}^{m+12} (y_{rt} - \hat{y}_t), \qquad \text{equation 4(a)}$$

$$s_E = s\sqrt{12 + 144/m + [144(\bar{\bar{x}} - \bar{x})^2 / \sum_{t=1}^{m} (x_t - \bar{x})^2]}$$

equation 4(b)

$$UCL_{1-\beta}(E) = \hat{E} + t_{1-\beta,m-2} \cdot s_E, \qquad \text{equation 4(c)}$$

where

$$s = \sqrt{\sum_{t=1}^{m} (y_t - \hat{y}_t)^2/(m - 2)}$$

$$\bar{\bar{x}} = \sum_{t=m+1}^{m+12} x_t/12$$

$$\bar{x} = \sum_{t=1}^{m} x_t/m$$

"t"$_{1-\beta,m-2}$ = the "t" table value for $1-\beta$ confidence and $m-2$ degrees of freedom.

Figure 10 shows the use of regression analysis on application number 64 of the data sets. It is a facsimile of a printout that an auditor might receive in an audit. The intolerable amount (E*) is assumed to be \$2. The base period y_t and x_t ($t = 1-36$) were used to get the estimates a = \$.27, b = \$1.99, and s = \$.517. The a and b are used along with x_{37} to x_{48} (x's for audit year months 1-12) to get $\hat{y}_t$ or the "Regression Estimated Value of y" and the $\hat{e}_t$ or the "Estimated Residual." The estimated total monetary error for the year ($\hat{E}$) is $Y_r - \hat{Y}$ or \$94.09 − \$92.96 = \$1.13. The s_E is computed as:

$$s_E = \$.517\sqrt{12 + \frac{144}{36} + \frac{144[(45.11/12) - (146.34/36)]^2}{19.61}}$$
$$= \$2.11$$

FIGURE 10
FACSIMILE AUDIT REGRESSION OUTPUT

BASE PERIOD SUMMARY DATA

ESTIMATED RELATIONSHIP : E(Y/X) = .27 + 1.99*X
SUM OF X : 146.34
STANDARD DEVIATION OF RESIDUALS : S = .517
SUM OF (X - XBAR)**2 : 19.61

APPLICATION NUMBER = 64 INTOLERABLE AMOUNT= 2.000

DETAILED AUDIT PERIOD DATA

MONTH NUMBER	VALUE OF X	BOOK VALUE OF Y	REGRESSION ESTIMATED VALUE OF Y	ESTIMATED RESIDUAL	STANDARD ERROR OF PREDICTION	CONFIDENCE FACTOR	UPPER CONFIDENCE LIMIT	INVESTIGATE ?
37	3.66	8.21	7.55	.67	.53	2.03	1.07	NO
38	4.11	7.74	8.45	-.71	.52	2.03	1.06	NO
39	3.30	6.76	6.83	-.07	.53	2.03	1.08	NO
40	3.58	7.22	7.39	-.17	.53	2.03	1.07	NO
41	4.08	8.23	8.39	-.16	.52	2.03	1.06	NO
42	3.95	9.44	8.12	1.32	.52	2.03	1.06	YES
43	4.20	8.43	8.62	-.19	.52	2.03	1.06	NO
44	2.88	5.93	6.00	-.07	.54	2.03	1.10	NO
45	3.66	7.62	7.55	.07	.53	2.03	1.07	NO
46	4.43	9.16	9.07	.09	.53	2.03	1.07	NO
47	4.21	8.88	8.63	.25	.52	2.03	1.06	NO
48	3.06	6.46	6.35	.11	.54	2.03	1.09	NO
YEAR	45.11	94.09	92.96	1.13	2.11	.256	1.67	NO

* STATISTICAL OUTLIER TEST FOR MONTHS---INVESTIGATE IF EST RESIDUAL) UCL;
ESTIMATED ERROR TEST FOR YEAR---INVESTIGATE IF UCL) INTOLERABLE AMOUNT

$UCL_{.60}$ (E) is computed as:

$$UCL_{.60}(E) = 1.13 + .256 \cdot \$2.11$$
$$= \$1.67.$$

For application 64 the auditor has .60 confidence that accounting error is no more than $1.67. (The rest of Figure 10 will be explained below.)

Note that the calculation of $UCL_{1-\beta}$ (E) is not affected by how actual accounting error might be spread among months. The $\hat{E}$ and s_E will be the same for *any* distribution of E* including the theoretically "most adverse" or "hardest to find" distribution. This property is desirable since unintentional accounting error may be distributed in a number of ways and intentional error may be purposely distributed in the "hardest to find" manner by those persons committing fraud.

As stated previously, if the $(1-\beta)$ upper confidence limit calculated using 4c is less than tolerable error (E*), the auditor will have evidence that accounting overstatement error is not material at the $1-\beta$ confidence level. If $UCL_{1-\beta}(E) \geq E^*$, then monthly balance tests can be applied as follow-up tests to identify the months most likely to contain monetary error.

Alternatively, if $UCL_{1-\beta}$ (E) is less than E*, the auditor may want to follow up with tests of individual months to identify extremely large monthly deviations. That is, even if the annual balance test indicates there is little risk that intolerable overstatement error exists for the year, a monthly scan may point out unusual conditions, operating problems, new equipment installation or production changes that may have significance to other parts of the audit. Such follow-up tests have considerable potential audit benefit and very low computation cost since the same regression analysis is used. We now turn to a description of a procedure for testing the individual monthly balances.

Monthly Balance Tests

Conceptually, the follow-up monthly balance test is similar to the annual balance test. The monthly balance test uses the results of regression analysis to compute an upper confidence limit (UCL) on accounting error in an account balance for each month of the audit period. However, there is no unique "intolerable amount" with which to compare a UCL by month. This lack of uniqueness is due to the fact that intolerable accounting error may be spread over the audit year in an infinite number of ways. As examples, E* may appear in any of the 12 months with zero in the others or E*/2 may appear in any two months, or E*/2 in one and E*/6 in three months. Also, understatement errors may partially offset overstatement errors of greater than E*. One month may have an error of 1.5 E* and two other months have error of $-.25$ E*.

Even though there is not a theoretically correct monthly calculation and comparison for the monthly follow-up test, we do know that for a given value of x_t, the larger the $\hat{e}_t$ the less likely it is that the amount is due to chance or random variation and the more likely it is due to accounting error. A reasonable approach then is to scan the $\hat{e}_t$ and investigate if the amount is "sufficiently improbable" under the assumption that there is no overstatement error in the month. "Sufficiently improbable" can be assessed by the product of the standard deviation of the monthly prediction error (s_{e_t}) and the "t" value that reflects the type I error risk (no error, but investigate). Since the monthly balance test involves type I error, we use $t_{1-\alpha}$ to denote this "t" value.

Thus, the mechanics of the follow-up monthly balance tests require estimates of accounting error for the month ($\hat{e}_t$), the standard deviation of monthly prediction error (s_{e_t}) and the choice of a confidence level ($1-\alpha$). The formulas for these estimates for each month t in the audit year (t = m + 1, m + 2, . . . , m + 12) are:

$$\hat{e}_t = y_{rt} - \hat{y}_t \qquad \text{equation 5(a)}$$

$$s_{e_t} = s\sqrt{1 + \frac{1}{m} + [x_t - \bar{x})^2 / \sum_{t=1}^{m} (x_t - \bar{x})^2]} \qquad \text{equation 5(b)}$$

An $\hat{e}_t$ that is greater than $s_{e_t} \cdot$ "t"$_{1-\alpha,\, m-2}$ is deemed to be "sufficiently" improbable (recall that the expectation of e_t is zero). Thus, y_{rt} would be investigated for possible overstatement error if $\hat{e}_t$ is greater than or equal to $s_{e_t} \cdot$ "t"$_{1-\alpha,\, m-2}$.

As stated above, there is no single monthly risk level that can be proven to limit risk to the annual risk level. However, for annual balance tests with $\beta = .40$, a monthly level of $\alpha = .05$ seems to give a reasonable tradeoff between signalling too many "false" investigations and too few "correct" investigations. That is, a "t" value for .05 risk or .95 confidence seems appropriate. This value is approximately 1.69. When the annual balance test indicates that an intolerable error is not likely, the auditor may still want to follow up with a monthly test of extreme values. For this purpose, we use $\alpha = .025$ or a "t" value of 2.03. Thus a month is more likely to be investigated if the annual balance test indicates that intolerable overstatement error may exist.

The numerical example shown in Figure 10 will help illustrate the approach and its characteristics. Assume that the auditor has decided to use the $\alpha = .05$ and $\alpha = .025$ rule as discussed in the previous paragraph. Consider month 37 which has a standard error of prediction (s_{e_t}) of approximately \$.53 and the estimated residual $\hat{e}_t = y_{r_t} - \hat{y}_t$ (i.e., the estimated unexplained monetary amount for the month) is \$.67. Since the annual balance test indicates that an intolerable overstatement is unlikely, the auditor would use a confidence factor of "t" = 2.03 to calculate $s_{e37} \cdot$ "t"$_{1-.025,34}$ or \$.53 · 2.03 = \$1.07. Since this is greater than $\hat{e}_t$ = \$.67, no investigation of month 37 is indicated.

If, on the other hand, the annual balance test had indicated that intolerable overstatement error is reasonably probable, "t"$_{1-.05,34}$ = 1.69 would be used and the auditor would calculate \$.53 · 1.69 = \$.90, and an investigation of month 37 would still not be indicated. Note that while a month with, say, $\hat{e}$ = \$.93, is not investigated for the first rule, it would be for the second. Also, $\hat{e}_t$ = \$1.50 would be investigated for either rule. That is, such a large $\hat{e}_t$ is deemed to be worthy of auditor follow-up even if intolerable error for the annual balance seems unlikely.

In Figure 10, accounting error of \$1.00 was seeded in months 42 and 44. Thus, the total is intolerably overstated and when combined with errors in other accounts may lead to a material misstatement of the statements as a whole. The annual balance test failed to indicate an investigation. Given that $\beta = .40$ was used in the annual balance test and a monthly follow-up was also applied, we would expect such annual type II errors on about 40 percent of such applications. However, the monthly outlier test did identify month 42 as being exceptionally large and needing investigation. The monthly outlier follow-up means that the auditor may still avoid unwarranted reduction of planned tests of details and thus avoid a type II error. Problems 4 and 5 below will give you some indication of how reliable the procedure is over repeated trials.

We have described how regression analysis can be used by the auditor in the analytical review of a client's income statement account. In particular, if the assumptions of the regression model are not violated, the auditor can use the analysis to formulate tests of the annual account balance and follow-up tests of the individual monthly balances. Research on the use of such annual balance and monthly balance tests over repeated trials in simulated environments suggests that actual rate of type II errors does not exceed the theoretical level (β) which was specified in formulating the tests.[3] Thus, the auditor

---

[3] See Kinney and Salamon [1982].

may be able to use regression to produce 1) *objective* and 2) *statistically valid* evaluations of client account balances. These two characteristics are important. Objectivity means that the technique can be more readily taught to new members of the audit firm and defended to others, and statistical validity means that the auditor's decision regarding the necessity (or lack of it) for detailed testing of the client's records can be logically defended should the need to do so arise. There is also some evidence that the auditor's overall understanding of a client's business is improved by follow-up investigations of large $\hat{e}_t$.

Regression Analysis Problems

Phase I—Analysis of a Single Fiscal Year

Phase I consists of three problems that test your ability to conduct an analytical review of an income statement account balance for a particular audit year. Each of you will probably receive a different audit year when you run REGRN. Consequently, you will have to work independently on this assignment. The computer will provide all necessary information about your client. All tests are for errors of overstatement.

-----You are now ready to solve problems 1, 2, and 3-----

Problem 1

Run REGRN problem 1 and select an audit year by entering the last four (right-most) digits of your social security number. CAARS will list and plot the base and audit period data for the year that your number indicates. The y_t values for 19A4 may have been seeded with overstatement error for one or more months.

Review the computer-generated printout of y_t and x_t values for the three years of audited data and for the current year's unaudited data and examine the associated scatterplot. (No calculations are required.)

(a) Does the account balance for the year under audit seem reasonable or does it seem to be unreasonably large? Explain. Assume that intolerable error for 19A4 is $2. Based on the data, how confident are you that the audited values for the year taken as a whole are not "intolerably" overstated? Explain.

(b) Does the account balance for any month of the audit period seem large enough to justify an examination of the details supporting that monthly balance? Explain the basis upon which your opinion was formed.

Problem 2

This problem uses residual plots to help you assess regression model validity. You are provided plots from two different applications of regression analysis. In each application, it is assumed that

$y_t = A + Bx_t + e_t$

and e_t is distributed NID(0, S^2)

In addition, ordinary least-squares regression has been run to find the estimates of A, B, and e_t.

Use the graph from the output for problem 2 and do the following.

(a) Examine the plots of $\hat{e}_t$ versus x_t and time (t) for the first application and answer the following questions:
   (1) Do the residual plots seem consistent or inconsistent with the assumptions of simple regression analysis? Explain.
   (2) What does the analysis in part (a) suggest to you about the relationship between y_t and x_t at high versus low volumes of x_t? Early versus late periods?
   (3) Would you be willing to use this regression model as a basis for conducting statistical evaluations of the client's reported annual balance? Explain.

(b) Repeat (a), parts (1), (2), and (3) for the second application.

Problem 3

In this problem you conduct annual and monthly balance overstatement tests for a particular audit year. You are provided with a computer printout which contains summary data regarding the relationship between a client's audit account balance (y) and an independent variable (x) for the 36 months prior to the current year—the year now under audit. In addition, the printout provides data on the book value of the account balance as well as the regression-estimated value of that balance for each month during the audit period as in Figure 10.

Unlike the printout in Figure 10, there is an incomplete

calculation of the UCLs—that is your job. Also, unlike Figure 10 (and unlike an application in practice) you are told where actual accounting error exists. Thus, you can tell whether application of regression analysis has led to a type I or type II error for each month and the year as a whole.

You have no reason to suspect that any of the assumptions of the regression model are violated and consequently, the regression model will be the basis for the analytical review of this account balance. You are willing to conduct your tests of the client's annual balance at an overall type II error risk level (β) of .40. That is, you want tests that will indicate intolerable error in the annual balance in 60 percent of those years in which intolerable error is present. In addition, you believe that an error of \$2 would be considered intolerable. CAARS has preset "t"$_{1-.40,34}$ = .256 and E* = \$2. Using the output for problem 3, complete the following:

(a) For month 2 of the audit period, verify the regression-estimated value of y (i.e., $\hat{y}_{38}$).

(b) Calculate the upper confidence limit on error for the year. What does this value for the upper confidence limit indicate about the annual balance? On the basis of the data, would you be justified in restricting planned tests of details on y for the audit year? If yes, what reliance would you place on analytical review?

(c) Calculate the appropriate comparison value (s_{e38} · "t"$_{1-\alpha,34}$) for month 38 (i.e., using $1-\alpha$ = .90 or .95). Is the $\hat{e}_{38} = y_{r38} - \hat{y}_{38}$ large enough to trigger a monthly follow-up investigation of the account for month 38?

(d) Repeat the procedures in (c) for month 42. Is the estimated error in month 42 sufficiently large to justify a follow-up investigation?

(e) Examine the results of the computer-generated *monthly* follow-up investigations and compare them to the distribution of accounting error in the audit period.

(1) How many type I errors were committed?

(2) How many type II errors (on a monthly basis) were committed?

(3) Did either your annual balance test or monthly follow-up tests indicate an investigation was needed?

Phase II—Analysis of 100 Years

Phase II consists of two problems that apply regression analysis to all 100 sets of audit years under different distributions of seeded error.

Problem 5 differs from problem 4 in that the correlation coefficient (but not the S factor) is altered. Again, all tests are for overstatement errors.

-----You are now ready to solve problems 4 and 5-----

Problem 4

In this problem you can assess the performance of regression in analytical review over repeated trials. Two sections of data are presented which deal with the repeated use of regression in analytical review. The first section provides summary data on regression model statistics of the estimation process for 100 simulated applications. Since this problem is based upon simulated data, it is known that the regression model assumptions are not violated.

The second section of data is concerned with the ability of the regression model to signal the presence of intolerable error in 100 simulated audit engagements. The 100 data sets differ as to whether intolerable error is or is not present in the audit year.

In addition, when intolerable error is present, the sets differ as to how the error is distributed across the months. Each line of output reflects results over 100 trials in which the same accounting error was seeded in each audit year month. The overall risk level (β) for the tests was set at .40.

After studying the output for problem 4, answer the following questions.

(a) The true value for the slope coefficient (B) in each of the regressions was 2.00. However, in 30 of 100 regressions the estimated slope coefficent is shown to be 1.94 or less. What might cause the estimated coefficients to be different than the true coefficient?

(b) The average value for the "R-square" associated with the regression is .90 over 100 trials. What is the meaning of R-square?

(c) For the case in which no error is seeded in the audit period, what is the number of monthly type I errors and the number of annual type I errors based upon the monthly balance test? Explain why the latter is smaller.

(d) Examine the case in which one-third of an intolerable error is seeded in three different months (line 4 of the table). Remember that 300 months (three months per year × 100 years) have accounting error seeded. Therefore, there may be as many as 300 monthly type II errors and as many as 900 monthly type I errors. For this case determine:

(1) How many months that have errors were investigated?
(2) How many months that have no errors were correctly treated (i.e., not investigated)?

(e) The type II error performance of the *monthly* balance follow-up test is not likely to be as good when the error is seeded in three or more months as it is when the error is seeded in one or two months. What do your results show?
   (1) Would an auditor be just as likely to use regression in analytical review for cases in which errors were contained in, say, four to six months as for those cases in which errors were contained in just one or two months? Explain.
   (2) How does the actual frequency of annual type II errors compare with the pre-specified risk level?

(f) (Optional) Repeat parts (c), (d), and (e) with alternative error amounts seeded and alternative levels of intolerable error or materiality. (Run problem 9 first.) What conclusions do you reach as to the ability of regression analysis to serve as a test-of-details substitute under differing levels of error?

Problem 5

This problem illustrates the effect of differing "statistical explanatory power" on error detection ability through a comparison with problem 4. The x_t, e_t, and accounting error seedings for problem 5 are identical to those of problem 4. The only difference is the true slope (B) which has been set to 1.0. This, in turn, changes the y_t values (since $y_t = A + B x_t + e_t$).

Use the output of problem 5 along with the output of problem 4 to answer the following questions:

(a) Compare the means and deciles of the estimates of R-square and the standard deviation of residuals (s) for problems 4 and 5. What is the effect of the true slope (B) on these estimates?

(b) Examine the error investigation performance statistics of the two problems. Do the regressions whose average R-square is lower perform better or worse in analytical review than the regression whose R-square is higher? Do you feel that you have more reliable audit evidence in the higher R-square case? Explain.

(c) Given your findings in (b), what can you say about the relevance of R-square as compared with the standard deviation of the residuals as an indicator of the ability of a regression model to serve as a substitute for test of details? Explain.

(d) What is the effect of the slope difference on the variance of y_t? (Hint: you can solve this by drawing some graphs or by using the relationship: $var(y_t) = B^2 var(x_t) + S^2$).

(e) Given your result in (d), do you agree with the following statement? "R-square measures the proportion of variation in y that is 'explained' by x, but the usefulness of a given R-square depends on the magnitude of variation in y *to be explained.*" Explain.

--Authors' Note--

If you wish to change the parameter of a problem or change the error seeding or the tolerable error amount, enter '9' when the program asks you to select a problem number. You may specify different A and B or may change S by entering "SEFACT" different from 1.0. CAARS changes S by multiplying each e_t by "SEFACT." You may also change the "t" value for the annual balance test as well as specify the amount and monthly distribution of error to be seeded. Finally, you can alter the amount deemed "intolerable" or material and you may select a particular year number for analysis (for problems 1-3). After you have made you selections, you will again be asked to enter a problem number (1-5).

REFERENCES

AICPA, "Codification of Auditing Standards and Procedures," *Statement on Auditing Standards,* No. 1 (AICPA, 1973).

———, "Segment Information," *Statement on Auditing Standards,* No. 21 (AICPA, 1977).

———, "Planning and Supervision," *Statement on Auditing Standards,* No. 22 (AICPA, 1978a).

———, "Analytical Review Procedures," *Statement on Auditing Standards,* No. 23 (AICPA, 1978b).

———, "Review of Interim Financial Information," *Statement on Auditing Standards,* No. 36 (AICPA, 1981).

———, "Audit Risk and Materiality," *Statement on Auditing Standards,* No. 47 (AICPA, 1983).

Arens, A. A. and J. K. Loebbecke, *Auditing: An Integrated Approach,* Second Edition (Englewood Cliffs, NJ: Prentice-Hall, Inc., 1980).

Coakley, J. R., and J. K. Loebbecke, "The Expectation of Accounting Errors in Medium-sized Manufacturing Firms," *Advances in Accounting* (1985), pp. 199-245.

Hylas, R. E. and R. H. Ashton, "Audit Detection of Financial Statement Errors," *The Accounting Review* (October 1982), pp. 751-765.

Kinney, W. R., Jr., "The Predictive Power of Limited Information in Preliminary Analytical Review: An Empirical Study," Supplement to the *Journal of Accounting Research* (1979), pp. 148-165.

———, and W. L. Felix, Jr., "Analytical Review Procedures," *The Journal of Accountancy* (October 1980), pp. 98-103.

———, and G. L. Salamon, "The Effect of Measurement Error on Regression Results in Analytical Review," *Symposium on Auditing Research III* (University of Illinois Trustees, 1978), pp. 49-64.

———, "Regression Analysis in Auditing: A Comparison of Alternative Investigation Rules," *Journal of Accounting Research* (Autumn 1982), pp. 350-366.

———, and W. C. Uecker, "Mitigating the Consequences of Anchoring in Auditor Judgments," *The Accounting Review* (January 1982), pp. 55-69.

Smith, D. G., *Analytical Review* (Toronto: Canadian Institute of Chartered Accountants, 1983).

Warren, C. S., "Materiality and Audit Risk-Survey Research: An Update," Unpublished paper, University of Georgia (April 21, 1983).

Appendix

Notes to Instructors

CAARS consists of three compiled Microsoft FORTRAN programs and three data files. The programs include CAARS which prints background information about the system and the RATIO and REGRN programs. The files include RATIO.DAT and REGRN.DAT which contain data for RATIO and REGRN and a file called PSWD. PSWD allows you to alter the seeding of error in RATIO problems 1, 2, and 3 and to control access to REGRN problem 7 which prints a solution to REGRN problem 3. The use of PSWD is described below and in an Authors' Note which is available to instructors upon request. (Note: Requests for the PSWD Authors' Note should be sent on a school or firm's letterhead stationery and signed by a faculty member or appropriate official. Requests should be sent to: CAARS, American Accounting Association, 5717 Bessie Drive, Sarasota, FL 33583.)

CAARS was designed to be used by students with minimal guidance from instructors. Accordingly, some parameters have been fixed to simplify set-up on the microcomputer. We do this to avoid start-up cost to you. The student can simply insert the diskette into a 256K IBM—PC or compatible machine, type in 'CAARS', and follow instructions provided on the screen. We have used the program by giving several CAARS floppy disks to the microcomputer lab monitor for students to check out or copy. The fact that CAARS needs no set-up instructions makes this possible and makes home use by off-campus students easy. We have also had the program stored on a controlled hard disk with equal success.

RATIO is programmed to seed the same error condition for *all* students for problems 1, 2, and 3. We have found class discussion to be much easier if all students have the same error seeded. The initial PSWD seeds omitted credit purchases. That is, the material amount for the year is computed and subtracted from the test month's Cost of Sales and ending Accounts Payable. If you want to change to seed no error or to add material fictitious credit sales, you must alter the PSWD file as described in the PSWD Authors' Note. If you want the students to experiment with errors of a different amount or type, they must individually execute problem *9* to change these parameters (See Authors' Note at the end of Chapter Two).

REGRN is programmed to seed errors of $.67 in months 38, 42, and 45 (i.e., E = \$2). Tolerable error (E*) is set at \$2.00 and "t" set at .256 (i.e., beta is .40). If you want the students to experiment with other error amounts, other distributions over months (problems 1-3), other E* values, other "t" values, or other regression parameter values (A, B, or S), they must execute problem *9* first (see Authors' Note at the end of Chapter Three).

We have found the fixed-parameter choices to be adequate for undergraduate classes and it has minimized instructor time. Advanced students wanting to experiment or test sensitivity to parameter choices will find the "problem 9" feature useful.

Chapters One and Two (without problems) can be assigned as advanced reading and covered in a single class period. Students can then be assigned the problems in Chapter Two as homework for the subsequent class period. If all or most of the problems in Chapter Two are assigned, a full class period will probably be required to go over the problems and to review the use of ratio analysis in analytical review.

Since financial ratio analysis seems to be most useful at the planning and final evaluation stages, we usually assign Chapters One and Two at the time audit planning or the "audit process overview" is being presented. We emphasize the use of ratio analysis as an attention director. Chapter Three is assigned immediately before monetary (or variables) sampling tests of details. Regression analysis is discussed as a test of details substitute. Chapter Three takes about a full class period. We introduce the subject by reviewing concepts of regression analysis at the end of the class period before Chapter Three is assigned.

In the notes below we offer teaching suggestions to instructors planning to use CAARS. The suggestions are based upon our use of CAARS in our auditing classes at the University of Iowa, the University of Michigan, and Rice University.

Teaching Suggestions

I. Introduction

Chapter One of CAARS is a general discussion of analytical review. We emphasize the following aspects of the chapter.

1. Definition of analytical review as a substantive test and contrast of it with tests of details.

2. Uses of analytical review. We ask students to consider the advantages and relative risks of using analytical review as an attention director vs. as a test-of-details substitute.
3. Timing of analytical review *vis-a-vis* its uses.
4. Methods of analytical review (Figure 2). Other classifications of methods are, of course, possible but we have found this one to be useful. We like to emphasize the cost of differential information and computation required as well as the ability to get "tight" and objective measures of dispersion along with the expectation. If you wish to emphasize audit judgment, the analytical review judgment exercise in Kinney and Uecker [1982, p. 58] can be used at this point to further illustrate the subjective method of analytical review.
5. Diagram of CAARS (Figure 3): We point out that the only inputs required of students are the rules and critical values. CAARS seeds the errors, uses the critical values to determine whether an investigation is warranted, and calculates the frequencies of type I and type II errors resulting from the use of the specified critical values. Thus CAARS permits students to focus on the important audit judgments of specification of rules and critical values with a minimum of data entry or calculation.

We emphasize the advantages of using seeded errors for evaluating a decision strategy. A practitioner often will not know that a strategy has led to a type II error until it is too late to correct it. With seeded errors we can see the effectiveness of a strategy and, in cases in which no error has been seeded, its efficiency.

II. Financial Ratio Analysis Module

Chapter Two of CAARS illustrates the use of ratio analysis in analytical review. Ratio analysis is appealing because it requires relatively little data and is easy to understand. However, as is demonstrated, ratio analysis is not very effective in detecting material error even in monthly account balances. Consequently, ratio analysis may be more appropriate for attention directing at the planning or final evaluation steps than as a test-of-details substitute.

Before assigning the problems in Chapter Two, we review the following material in the text:

1. The types of accounting errors that could be seeded and their predicted effect on the four ratios employed (see Figure 4). We do

not tell students in advance that the same error type has been seeded for all of them.

2. For the *ad hoc* and univariate statistical investigation rules, we alert students to the one-sided nature of the test to determine whether an investigation for overstatement of earnings is warranted. Specifically, CAARS signals an investigation for Accounts Receivable Turnover and the Accruals Ratio if the computed test statistic is greater than the critical value specified by the student. For the Inventory Turnover and the Cost of Sales Ratio, CAARS signals an investigation if the computed test statistic is less than the specified critical value.
3. We warn students that normal variation in a ratio (noise) can lead to the situation that a ratio may change in the opposite direction of that predicted for a particular material error. For example, Accounts Receivable Turnover may decrease in the test month even though a material fictitious credit sale has been seeded. It is the normal variation in most ratios combined with the fact that a material amount may be relatively small in relation to an account balance which limits the usefulness of ratio analysis in detecting material accounting error.
4. Pattern analysis. We discuss the error time-series plots of Figure 5, pointing out the self-correcting nature of some errors for some ratios and the fact that some ratios are more sensitive to the presence of accounting error than others. It is important to note that Figure 5 is based on monthly data with the material amount for the year seeded in one month. The sensitivity of the ratios to the presence of material accounting error using annual balance data will typically be much lower.

Below we describe the RATIO problems and offer suggestions for their expansion.

Problem 1

The purpose of the first problem is to give students an opportunity to use a purely subjective approach to analytical review. Problem 1 uses monthly data and we remind the students that a quick and easy analysis of *annual* balances will be much less effective in error detection. Some students will be able to detect the error seeded (e.g., material omitted purchases on account), but many will not; there are many "outlier" months in which "noise" hides the seeded error even for "annual" material error in a single monthly statement.

You may want to have the students increase the magnitude of the error seeded (by running problem 9) immediately after they complete problem 1. By exercising this option, students can verify their hypothesis of the error seeded by specifying that, say, four or five times the material amount of error be seeded. If their initial hypothesis concerning which error was seeded was correct, the ratios should exhibit the same, but more pronounced, pattern as before.

Note: For simplicity, RATIO allows only months 2-12 as test months. This skirts the conceptual question of whether a possible comparison of January's book values with audited values of the previous December is inherently more reliable than a comparison of, say, February's book values with January's book values.

Problem 2

The second problem extends the subjective analysis in problem 1 to the use of prespecified objective investigation rules. One approach to problem 2 is to ask students to use both rules, running the problem once for each rule. Since the omitted purchase error will also be present in problem 2, students are encouraged to use their prior knowledge in specifying critical values under either rule. In addition to the question in the text for problem 2, students can be asked which of the two rules seems easier to apply and which rule makes more correct decisions for their test month. We also ask the students to consider the computation cost (rule 2 requires the calculation of the standard deviation estimate (s) using the previous year's audited ratios while rule 1 doesn't).

Problem 3

The third problem repeats independently the seeding and analysis in problem 2 (the same omitted purchases error is seeded) for each of the 11 remaining months of the test year as well as for the other three audit years. The objective of this problem is to give students some perspective on the overall effectiveness of a particular investigation rule as conditions change over time. Students are encouraged again to compare two rules to determine whether the rule that seemed to work better for a single test month in problem 2 also works better over repeated trials. This prevents students from developing excessive and unwarranted confidence in a particular rule that works well in one month's situation but not others. That is, the students might pick extremely small critical values in order to signal the error in a particular month. (This excessive investigation problem is further clarified in problem 4 when no error or a different error is present.)

If time permits, we recommend that students be instructed to choose the rule that seems to work best over all years for the particular error condition and attempt to improve its performance by revising the critical values. Since a rule must be applied under uncertainty over conditions of different types of error and error of different amounts, we also refer to the results of problem 4 to help discussion of audit policy-setting, and particularly the need to consider the "Inherent Risk" (*SAS No. 47*, par. 20) or "prior probability" of errors of various types and amounts.

We like to point out that a signal to investigate a ratio does not automatically identify which account may be in error. For example, inventory overstatement affects only the numerator of the Cost of Sales Ratio. Consequently, a correct decision to investigate the ratio is correct only for the numerator of the ratio. For the denominator, a type I error would result. Thus the frequency of type I and type II errors tabulated by CAARS understates the actual number on an account basis because each ratio involves two accounts. An especially valuable lesson for students is that even with no error some individual months will show large deviations and vice versa. Over all periods, however, regularity prevails. Students can develop an appreciation for the fact that the law of large numbers doesn't apply to a sample of one (month) yet they see that it does apply on a sample of, say, 48. We find that problems 3 and 4 provide a good start for a discussion of the implications of the law of large numbers for audit risk and an audit firm's policy setting.

Problem 4

This problem provides the broadest basis for developing an assessment of the effectiveness of a particular rule or rules. All three error conditions (no error, omitted purchase, and fictitious sale) are alternately seeded to all 48 months and the student-specified investigation rule applied. Because the "no error" condition is also represented in this problem, students are forced to consider the trade-offs between type I and type II errors in assessing the effectiveness of a particular rule.

The reliability of the pattern measure in this problem is interesting. While the pattern measure is rather effective in indicating error when it exists (at least for monthly data), it is, of course, somewhat less accurate in identifying the type of error. This results from the fact that a particular ratio may be affected in the same way by several different errors. For example, the Cost of Sales and Accrual Ratios each change in the same direction in response to either an omitted purchase or a fictitious sale (see Figure 4).

Problems 3 and 4 are both useful in discussing audit policy-setting and the role of inherent risk.

Problem 5

This problem illustrates how an auditor can employ microcomputer-generated output as a decision aid to test alternative explanations for an unusual fluctuation. The error seeded is an omitted purchase but the client attributes the decrease in the Cost of Sales Ratio to a special sale in the test month that generated an unusually high contribution margin. Problem 5 illustrates how the auditor could test the client's explanation by "backing out" the entries that *would have been* caused by the special sale. If the client's explanation is correct, this procedure should bring the ratios into closer conformity to their expected values, i.e., closer to zero in the standardized output plot. However, if the client's explanation is not correct, the procedure should have the opposite effect.

Most students' solutions will exhibit a more dispersed distribution of points when the controller's solution is plotted, and a narrower distribution for the correct answer. Again, however, some plots are not well behaved.

III. Regression Analysis Module

The purpose of the single-year problems (1-3) is to give students some experience in applying time-series regression to a specific audit year. The 100-year problems (4-5) provide summary data from 100 replications. These problems enable students to see how well regression performs over many trials that are the same as to underlying parameters and differ only as to random variation components (i.e., x_t and e_t).

In introducing regression analysis in auditing, we remind students that they must assess the expected audited values and a reasonable range of audited values given their information and model. Their information includes the base period y_t, audit period y_{rt}, and the base and audit period x_t values. We have found the diagram in Figure A.1 useful for illustrating the origins of the quantities underlying equations 4(a), 4(b), and 4(c) in Chapter Three.

FIGURE A.1
DIAGRAM OF REGRESSION DATA AND ESTIMATES

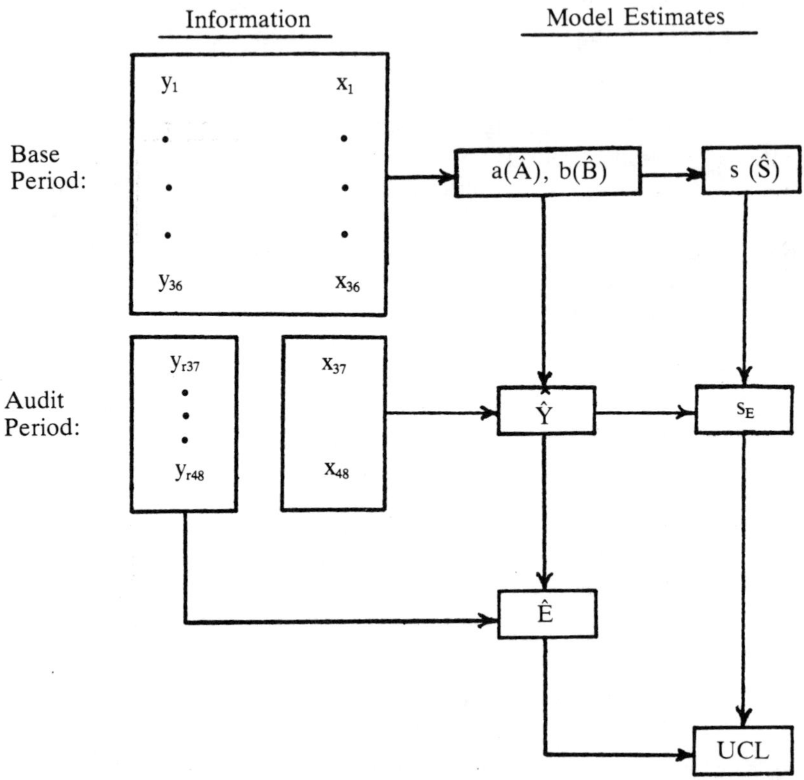

Problem 1

Problem 1 requires no calculation. Its purpose is to show how difficult it is to decide subjectively whether an annual or monthly balance might contain a material error based on the data alone. REGRN has seeded \$.67 errors in months 38, 42, and 45 for a total of \$2 which is also the "intolerable amount" (E*). Output interpretation (keyed to questions):

a. The errors are particularly difficult to see in a scanning of the list of the monthly y and x data. However, if one merely compares the total Y and X values for each of the four years, it is usually the case that the book Y_r for the audit period is larger than audited Y for the other three years. It is also true that the audit period X is about the same as for the three base-period years. This is because \$.67 has been added to each of three "audited" y values to get Y_r. The x values for all come from the same distribution for both the base and audit periods. Consequently, it appears to many students that the annual balance for the year under audit might contain a material error. It is still difficult to assess subjectively how confident one should be.

b. A scan of the monthly account printout for the audit period does not seem to be revealing. The largest values for y_r seem to occur in the months with the largest values for x. However, it is true that the larger y_r values for the audit year tend to occur in months 38, 42, and 45 even when their x values aren't among the largest.

c. A scan of the scatter plot usually doesn't show the audit period values to be "out of line" with the base-period relationship. However, one or more of the months actually seeded with error usually tends to be among the highest. We discuss the fact that the example error of \$.67 is just a little more than the (monthly) standard deviation (S) of \$.50. Thus, the error signal to noise ratio is not particularly high for an error of E*/3.

d. The scatter plot shows how knowledge of the x series aids the auditor in the evaluation of the y_r series even when a formal regression model is not utilized since the x,y plot shows months 38, 42, and 45 are often "on the high side."

e. Since the scatter plot is somewhat useful in assessing possible error, we also discuss how the visual analysis would become more complicated if the auditor were to use multiple x_t series and multiple regression.

Problem 2

This problem allows the instructor to bring up issues regarding base-period regression model validity. While this problem is termed a single-year problem, it provides plots of base-period residuals from two related regression applications. In one of these applications the intercept of the regression is different in the first 18 months of the base period than it is in the second 18 months of the period. The student's social security number is used to determine whether the first or the second application is the one with the assumption violation.

The plot of residuals ($\hat{e}_t$) versus x_t for both applications seems to be consistent with what we would expect if the regression assumptions hold. That is, the deviations are centered at about zero and have about the same vertical "spread" for all values of x_t. The same relationship holds for one of the plots of $\hat{e}_t$ against the month number (t). However, the plot of residuals versus time does not seem consistent with the assumptions for one of the applications. In particular, the first 18 residuals are predominantly negative (positive) while the last 18 are predominantly positive (negative). Thus, it does not appear that the expected value of the residuals is zero for all values of t as is assumed in regression analysis.

For this application, the model which generated the data was:

$$y_t = \$-.42 + \$2x_t + e_t, \text{ (if } 1 \leq t \leq 18),$$
$$y_t = \$1.08 + \$2x_t + e_t, \text{ (if } 18 < t \leq 36).$$

Therefore, the intercept is different in the last 18 months than the first 18 months. You may find it beneficial to mention this to students when this problem is discussed. We discuss possible reasons for a change in the intercept.

The simple regression model for one case cannot be relied upon to produce valid statistical inferences about the client's reported balances because it is apparent that the simple regression assumptions do not hold in the application. Furthermore, it is instructive at this point to introduce the concept of a dichotomous or "dummy" variable and to discuss how the introduction of the dummy variable into the simple regression model can account for this intercept change. The other application does not violate and usually does not appear to violate any of the assumptions associated with the simple regression model. Therefore, the model should lead to valid statistical inferences regarding the client's reported balances.

Problem 3

This problem is aimed at developing the student's understanding of the mechanics of the monthly balance test and the annual balance test. To illustrate, we usually copy the output for a test application (other than no. 64) and walk through the calculations based on the output from problem 3. Specifically, we show how to calculate $\hat{E}$, s_E, and the UCL for the year along with the monthly follow-up for one month. Implications of the signals for audit follow-up are then discussed.

To help in verifying calculations, one can get a printed solution to problem 3 by running problem 7 and entering the "six-digit solution code." This causes the computer to print a solution to problem 3 for the next social security number entered (or the conditions set by having run problem 9). For the initial value stored in PSWD, the number '122816' will allow access. If after announcing that number you want to end student access, you must alter the PSWD file. The PSWD Authors' Note, available to instructors upon request, describes the nature of the PSWD file, how to change it, and how to select a new PSWD amount and the formula to compute the related 'solution code.' (It should be noted that students with knowledge of the initial value in PSWD may reenter the initial value and continue to use 122816.)

Since the data for problem 3 have intolerable error seeded, we discuss whether the annual balance test indicated possible overstatement and ask students how their applications turned out. About 40 percent will say that the annual balance test missed the error. Again we discuss audit risk and policy-setting over a large number of audits.

We also discuss the monthly follow-up tests and whether there was some indication of error in the annual or monthly balance tests. Only about 20 percent will say that both tests failed. We also discuss the fact that discovering and correcting even \$.67 will, in this case, make the annual error less than an intolerable amount (\$2.).

Problem 4

The purpose of this problem is to let the student see how regression performs in detecting errors in repeated applications under various error seedings. The pre-set data for this problem have $E = E^*$ = \$2. Since every student gets all 100 applications, their answers are the same. Because of this, we have printed the output for problems 4 and 5 (see Figures A.2 and A.3). If pressed for time, you may find it beneficial not to assign problems 4 and 5 as homework, but rather print copies of the solutions and discuss them in class. Problem 4 will take about two minutes to execute.

FIGURE A.2
OUTPUT FOR REGRN PROBLEM 4

BASE PERIOD
REGRESSION STATISTICS
SUMMARY FROM 100 TRIALS

PROBLEM 4

TRUE RELATIONSHIP: E(Y/X) = .33 + 2.00 *X

	AVERAGE VALUE	DISTRIBUTION DECILES .1	.2	.3	.4	.5	.6	.7	.8	.9
ESTIMATED ALPHA	.33	-.24	-.01	.12	.23	.33	.42	.63	.71	.85
ESTIMATED BETA	2.00	1.88	1.90	1.93	1.98	2.00	2.03	2.05	2.10	2.15
R-SQUARE	.90	.86	.88	.89	.90	.91	.91	.92	.93	.94
STANDARD DEVIATION OF RESIDUALS	.49	.41	.43	.46	.48	.50	.51	.53	.54	.57

100 YEAR SUMMARY OF INVESTIGATIONS

PROBLEM 4

THE AMOUNT OF ERROR SEEDED IN THE AUDIT PERIOD IS 2.000

THE AMOUNT OF ERROR CONSIDERED TO BE INTOLERABLE IS 2.000

ERROR CONDITION	# OF YEARS ANNUAL BALANCE TEST INDICATES POSSIBLE INTOL. ERROR	TOTAL MONTHS INVESTIGATED	# OF YEARS WITH AT LEAST ONE MONTH INVESTIGATED	MONTHLY INVESTIGATION ERRORS TYPE I	TYPE II	NUMBER OF YEARS WITH INVESTIGATION FAILURES * (M)	(MY)
NO ERROR SEEDED	18	26	21	26	0		
ESEED/ 1 IN 1 MONTH(S)	62	132	98	34	2	2	2
ESEED/ 2 IN 2 MONTH(S)	62	144	82	31	87	22	15
ESEED/ 3 IN 3 MONTH(S)	62	133	75	30	197	33	21
ESEED/ 6 IN 6 MONTH(S)	62	101	68	15	514	36	23
ESEED/12 IN 12 MONTH(S)	62	82	58	0	1118	42	30

* M INDICATES YEARS IN WHICH TESTS BY MONTH FAILED TO FIND ANY ACCOUNTING ERROR

MY INDICATES YEARS IN WHICH BOTH TESTS BY MONTH FAILED TO FIND SEEDED ACCOUNTING ERROR AND THE ANNUAL BALANCE TESTS FAILED TO INDICATE POSSIBLE ACCOUNTING ERROR

FIGURE A.3
OUTPUT FOR REGRN PROBLEM 5

BASE PERIOD
REGRESSION STATISTICS
SUMMARY FROM 100 TRIALS

PROBLEM 5

TRUE RELATIONSHIP: E(Y/X) = .33 + 1.00 *X

	AVERAGE VALUE	.1	.2	.3	.4	.5	.6	.7	.8	.9
		DISTRIBUTION DECILES								
ESTIMATED ALPHA	.33	-.24	-.01	.12	.23	.33	.42	.63	.71	.85
ESTIMATED BETA	1.00	.88	.90	.93	.98	1.00	1.03	1.05	1.10	1.15
R-SQUARE	.69	.57	.63	.66	.69	.70	.73	.75	.77	.79
STANDARD DEVIATION OF RESIDUALS	.49	.41	.43	.46	.48	.50	.51	.53	.54	.57

100 YEAR SUMMARY OF INVESTIGATIONS

PROBLEM 5

THE AMOUNT OF ERROR SEEDED IN THE AUDIT PERIOD IS 2.000

THE AMOUNT OF ERROR CONSIDERED TO BE INTOLERABLE IS 2.000

ERROR CONDITION	# OF YEARS ANNUAL BALANCE TEST INDICATES POSSIBLE INTOL. ERROR	TOTAL MONTHS INVESTIGATED	# OF YEARS WITH AT LEAST ONE MONTH INVESTIGATED	MONTHLY INVESTIGATION ERRORS TYPE I	TYPE II	NUMBER OF YEARS WITH INVESTIGATION FAILURES * (M)	(MY)
NO ERROR SEEDED	18	26	21	26	0		
ESEED/ 1 IN 1 MONTH(S)	62	132	98	34	2	2	2
ESEED/ 2 IN 2 MONTH(S)	62	144	82	31	87	22	15
ESEED/ 3 IN 3 MONTH(S)	62	133	75	30	197	33	21
ESEED/ 6 IN 6 MONTH(S)	62	101	68	15	514	36	23
ESEED/12 IN 12 MONTH(S)	62	82	58	0	1118	42	30

* M INDICATES YEARS IN WHICH TESTS BY MONTH FAILED TO FIND ANY ACCOUNTING ERROR

MY INDICATES YEARS IN WHICH BOTH TESTS BY MONTH FAILED TO FIND SEEDED ACCOUNTING ERROR AND THE ANNUAL BALANCE TESTS FAILED TO INDICATE POSSIBLE ACCOUNTING ERROR

Output Interpretation (keyed to questions):

a) The estimated coefficients in any application will differ from the "true coefficients" because of the sampling error introduced by the noise component (e_t) of the regression model. Note that on average over the 100 trials the estimates of the intercept, slope, and standard deviation values are about equal to the true values (A = \$.3333, B = \$2. and S = \$.50). This shows that the regression estimates are unbiased.

b) Since the regression contains an intercept term, the R-square value can be interpreted as the percentage variation in the dependent variable which is explained by the regression model. R-square is often suggested as a criterion for evaluating how well the regression model "fits" the data. (See problem 5, however, for some insight into which characteristic of a regression model is important in the context of analytical review.)

c) This difference is caused by the fact that the 26 monthly investigations take place in only 21 different years.

d) It is useful to summarize the results in the following manner for the case of E/3 in each of three months:

		Intolerable Error Present in Monthly Balance		
		Yes	No	Total
Monthly Balance	Investigation	103	30 (Type I errors)	133
Test Results	No Investigation	197 (Type II errors)	870	1067
		300	900	1200

As was the case in the RATIO module, many students receive an application year in which intolerable error is not signaled even though it exists. This is disturbing to those students. Problem 4 gives some confidence that the Law of Large Numbers and the Central Limit Theorem are correct. The students develop an appreciation of the meaning of audit risk as a concept, which means that some percentage of audits will fail to detect an existing material error and that this risk can be reduced only by increasing type I errors or by a costly extension of audit procedures. In other words, this exercise helps students internalize the idea that auditing involves an explicit trade-off between type I and type II errors and the cost of doing more audit work, and the trade-off should be based on the assessed relative costs of these factors. This means, of course, that some type II errors will occur by explicit design and their occurrence does not necessarily arise because of audit "mistakes."

Problem 5

This problem demonstrates that the R-square statistic is not nearly as important to the auditor as is the relation between the amount of error considered to be intolerable (E*) and the standard error of the regression(s).

Suggested responses to problem 5 follow (keyed to questions):

a) The effect of $B=1$ is to reduce R-square and of course b, but to leave S (and s, and thus the relative UCLs) unchanged.
b) An examination of the two tables suggests that these regressions have audit performance that is exactly the same over the 100 years. They commit the same number of type I and type II errors. Notice that the two sets of regressions do not differ at all with respect to their standard errors even though they do differ as to their distribution of R-square.
c) The auditor wants to detect a certain dollar amount of error if it exists. This means that the important characteristic of a regression model is the size of its standard error in relation to the amount of error which is considered material—both s_e and E* are measured in dollars. The value for R-square (a proportion explained measure) is not of prime concern.
d) A graph will show a lower slope that greatly reduces the unconditional variation and range of the y_t values (see Figure A.4). Algebraically, since var(x) and S^2 are unchanged, the average effect is to reduce the first component of variance (B^2 var (x)) by reducing B^2 from 4 to 1.
e) Yes. The auditor needs an explanation in dollars, not percentages. For a given level of var(y) and degrees of freedom the auditor would, of course, prefer the model that gives the largest R-square (and equivalently, the smallest s).

FIGURE A.4
GRAPHS COMPARING MODELS IN PROBLEMS 4 AND 5

panel a. $y_t = \$.33 + \$2. x_t + e_{t1}$ ($e \sim NID(\$0, .5^2)$)

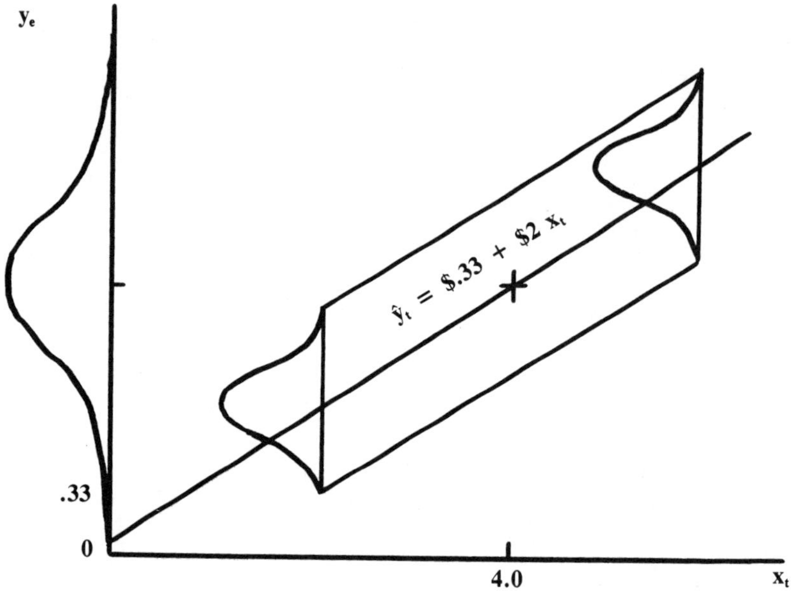

panel b. $y_t = \$.33 + \$1. x_t + e_t$ ($e \sim NID(\$0, .5^2)$)

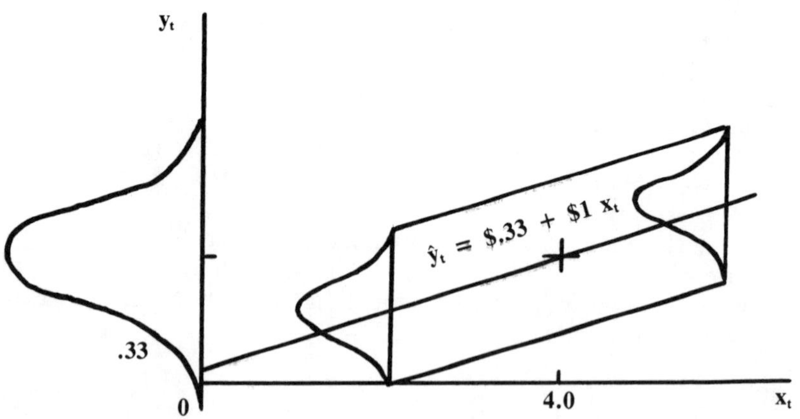